John Milton Paradise Lost, Book 1...

John Milton

PARADISE LOST

BOOK I.

GORSE

John Milton

PARADISE LOST

BOOK I.

EDITED

WITH LIFE, INTRODUCTION, NOTES, &c.

BY

F. GORSE, M.A.

SECOND MASTER, PARMITER'S FOUNDATION SCHOOL, LONDON

LONDON

BLACKIE & SON, LIMITED, 50 OLD BAILEY, E.C.

GLASGOW AND DUBLIN

1895

BLACKIE'S JUNIOR SCHOOL SHAKESPEARE.

In F'cap 8vo volumes, cloth limp.

The Merchant of Venice. Edited by GEORGE H. ELY, B.A., sometime Assistant Master in the United Westminster Schools. 112 pp., price 8d.

King Henry the Eighth. By the same Editor. 128 pp., price 8d.

As You Like It. Edited by LIONEL W. LYDE, M.A., sometime Exhibitioner of Queen's College, Oxford; Head English Master in Glasgow Academy. 120 pp., price 8d.

King Henry the Fifth. Edited by W. BARRY, B.A., English Master at Tettenhall College, Staffordshire. 128 pp., price 8d.

King Richard the Second. By the same Editor. 128 pp., price 8d.

Coriolanus. Edited by WALTER DENT. 158 pp., price 10d.

Julius Cæsar. By the same Editor. 112 pp., price 8d.

A Midsummer Night's Dream. Edited by W. F. BAUGUST, Chief Master of Modern Subjects in the United Westminster Schools. 96 pp., price 8d.

The Tempest. Edited by ELIZABETH LEE, Lecturer in English Literature at the Streatham Hill High School. 104 pp., price 8d.

King John. Edited by F. E. WEBB, B.A., sometime Scholar of Queen's College, Oxford. 112 pp., price 8d.

Hamlet. Edited by L. W. LYDE, M.A. Price 10d.

Twelfth Night. Edited by ELIZABETH LEE. Price 8d.

PREFATORY NOTE.

This edition aims at being a practical school book, providing all that is likely to be required by pupils in school, and at the same time free from the detail which can only usefully find a place in a book intended for more advanced students. Etymological matter has been but sparingly introduced, and the custom of quoting parallel passages from the ancient classics, so useful to the mature scholar but so bewildering to the young pupil, has been all but given up.

F. G.

January, 1895.

CONTENTS.

INTRODUCTION.

LIFE OF MILTON.

After Shakespeare, Milton is usually acknowledged to be the greatest English poet; yet he is not generally thought of as a national poet—as a representative of English character, in nearly the same degree as Shakespeare. He was closely connected with a *party*—the Puritans; and his eager partisanship undoubtedly had a narrowing effect upon him, and upon his later poetry. But was Milton a Puritan? He lived at a time when every man felt bound to take his stand with one of two parties: either with a king who was exercising despotic power in religious and civil matters; or with those who held that the king was bound to rule lawfully for the common good, and that in religion reasonable freedom should be allowed—whose motto was 'fair play' for everyone, even from kings. These principles Milton held as firmly as any man; to this extent he was one of the most earnest of Puritans. But it seems to be the very irony of fate, that he who took so keen a part in the struggle for freedom—freedom in religion, freedom from kingly tyranny, and freedom to think for one's self—now the most envied and the most cherished possessions of Englishmen, should not be more generally remembered and honoured as a great patriot. That he was not even a greater poet than he was, is due to the unhappy times in which he lived, and to the fact that, much as he loved poetry, he loved his country more.

The Milton family appear to have been distinguished by their strong convictions, and by their courage in acting upon them. The poet's grandfather is said to have been a staunch Catholic in the days of Elizabeth, and to have been heavily fined as a recusant—that is, for refusing to attend the services at the parish church. His son, the poet's father, on the other hand, became a Protestant, and was in consequence disinherited. He settled in London as a scrivener,[1] and prospered, and there the poet was born in 1608. His education was carried on at home by various masters, and by his father, who taught him to sing and to play the organ, and implanted in him his own love of music. Although his home was a cheerful and happy place, he seems to have been an unusually quiet, serious child, and prematurely studious, if we may judge from some lines placed by the engraver under a portrait of him, made when he was ten years old:

> "When I was yet a child, no childish play
> To me was pleasing: all my mind was set
> Serious to learn and know, and thence to do
> What might be public good; myself I thought
> Born to that end, born to promote all truth,
> All righteous things". (*Paradise Regained.*).

At twelve he was sent to St. Paul's School, quite near his home in the city of London, and he still had tutors at home. He now worked very hard indeed[2] for several years; no trouble or expense was grudged by his parents; for they were very proud of him, and had formed the highest hopes as to his future. In 1625, when in his seventeenth year, he entered Christ's College, Cambridge, and remained there till he was twenty-three.

Here came a break in his education, and with it the question, What was he going to do in life? His parents had destined him for the church; but the system of government by bishops and the tyranny of Laud deterred him from entering the ministry. His father seems to have left him free to choose a calling for himself,[3] and so we find him, about the

[1] The business of a scrivener in London consisted in the drawing up of wills, marriage settlements, and other deeds, the lending out of money for clients, and much else now done partly by attorneys, and partly by law-stationers.

[2] "My father destined me, while yet a little boy, for the study of humane letters, which I seized with such eagerness that from the twelfth year of my age I scarce ever went from my lessons to bed before midnight, which indeed was the first cause of injury to my eyes, to whose natural weakness there were also added frequent headaches."

[3] The elder Milton was himself a very well-educated man, and showed throughout the most generous sympathy and appreciation. The poet gratefully acknowledges this in his Latin poem *Ad Patrem*,—and hopes that other fathers may imitate him.

time of his leaving college, finally determined to fit himself, by continued labour and study, and by a strictly pure and blameless life, to achieve some great work as a poet. Accordingly he now settled at Horton, a quiet hamlet in Buckinghamshire, within a short distance of Windsor and the Thames, in the house of his father, who had retired thither to spend his old age.

Of the poems which he had already written the chief was *The Nativity Hymn*, begun on Christmas - day, 1629. His sonnet *On Arriving at his 23rd Year* is of special interest at this point:

" How soon hath Time, the subtle thief of youth,
    Stolen on his wing my three-and-twentieth year!
    My hasting days fly on with full career,
But my late spring no bud or blossom shew'th.
Perhaps my semblance might deceive the truth
    That I to manhood am arrived so near;
    And inward ripeness doth much less appear,
Than some more timely-happy spirits endu'th.
    Yet, be it less or more, or soon or slow,
It shall be still in strictest measure even
    To that same lot, however mean or high,
Toward which Time leads me, and the will of Heaven;
    All is, if I have grace to use it so,
    As ever in my great Task-Master's eye".

He seems to have devoted himself to an extensive course of 'select reading', especially to a revision of classical and Italian literature, storing his mind with all that was best worth appropriating, and becoming almost as familiar with Latin, Greek, and Italian as with his native tongue. He did not write more than five English poems of any great length during this period—*L'Allegro, Il Penseroso, Arcades, Comus,* and *Lycidas* — but they are amongst the very best in the language: and yet, in the last and the best of them, he is still dissatisfied with his powers. In the spring of 1637 he had lost his mother; next spring he started off to see Italy and Greece, which for him would be exceptionally interesting. But the tyranny of Charles had at last provoked his subjects in Scotland to rebellion. On hearing of this in South Italy,

PARADISE LOST.

Milton at once resolved to return and take his part with his countrymen in the impending contest.[1] In 1639 he was back. He took a house in London, and settled there for the rest of his life.[2]

So far Milton's life had been one of quiet, secluded study. For the next twenty years poetry was banished, study and self-preparation were all but given up, and he was to be found in the very thick of the controversies of the day,—writing against Episcopacy, defending the Execution of Charles (in two books—*the First* and *the Second Defence*), and exposing the notorious *Eikon Basilikè*. He had, on settling in London, begun to take a few pupils; this led him to write an essay on *Education*. But his only great and enduring work in prose was his *Areopagitica*, a plea for freedom of opinion, and for freedom to express that opinion to all the world by means of the printing-press, without the previous sanction of the Licenser. His activity in the Parliamentary cause had led to his being appointed, in 1649, Latin Secretary to the Committee of Foreign Affairs, a post for which his knowledge of foreign languages specially qualified him. It was during his tenure of this office that he deliberately hastened his blindness, which had been coming on for some years, over the writing of the *First Defence*, mentioned above.[3]

It is evident that this must have been, in his case, a terrible calamity, for he had not yet even begun his great poem. The truly admirable way in which he bore it is shown by the courage and patience which characterised his subsequent life,

[1] "I considered it," he says, "dishonourable to be enjoying myself at my ease in foreign lands, while my countrymen were striking a blow for freedom.

"I perceived that, if I ever wished to be of use, I ought at least not to be wanting to my country, to the church, and to so many of my fellow-Christians, in a crisis of so much danger; I therefore determined to relinquish the other pursuits in which I was engaged, and to transfer the whole force of my talents and my industry to this important object."

[2] Except during the plague in 1665-6, when he retired to Chalfont St. Giles, a village in Buckinghamshire, about 10 miles from Horton.

[3] "In such a case I could not listen to the physician, not if Æsculapius himself had spoken from his sanctuary; I could not but obey that inward monitor, I know not what, that spoke to me from Heaven. . . . I concluded to employ the little remaining eyesight I was to enjoy in doing this, the greatest service to the common weal it was in my power to render." (*Second Defence.*)

and by the various references to it which we find in his writings.[1]

But there were other misfortunes in store for him: in 1660 the Parliamentary cause failed completely — for the time; Milton was imprisoned, some of his prose writings were burnt by the hangman, and he lost most of his savings. He had indeed "fallen on evil days", and yet he bravely took up and carried to completion the great work of his life—his epic poem,[2] *Paradise Lost*. He had begun it before the Restoration, probably in 1658; he finished it about 1663, spent two years or so on its revision, and published it in 1667. Meanwhile he had commenced its sequel, *Paradise Regained*; then he wrote *Samson Agonistes*, a dramatic poem, and several prose works.

His latter years were greatly cheered and brightened by the fame which *Paradise Lost* brought him, and by the frank recognition of his pre-eminence by all parties.[3] He died in London in 1674, and was buried in the church of St. Giles, Cripplegate.

Three qualities stand out conspicuously in Milton's character. First, his deep sense of duty. He seems never to falter in his entire devotion to that which he believes he ought to do at any particular juncture. Two striking instances of this are, the return from Italy in 1639, and the employment of

---

[1] Cyriack, this three years' day these eyes, though clear,
    To outward view, of blemish or of spot,
    Bereft of light, their seeing have forgot;
Nor to their idle orbs doth sight appear
Of sun, or moon, or star, throughout the year,
    Of man, or woman. Yet I argue not
    Against Heaven's hand or will, nor bate a jot
Of heart or hope, but still bear up and steer
    Right onward. What supports me, dost thou ask?
The conscience, friend, to have lost them overplied
    In Liberty's defence, my noble task,
Of which all Europe rings from side to side.
    This thought might lead me through the world's vain mask
Content, though blind, had I no better guide.

[2] It may be noted here that *Paradise Lost* was at first intended to be written in the form of a drama.

[3] Dryden, the Royalist poet, admired Milton greatly, and with his leave adapted *Paradise Lost* for dramatic performance!

his failing eyesight in writing the *Defence*. Second, the sincerity and the earnestness of his religious and political convictions. Third, his magnanimity and patience. Twenty years spent in a cause that, for the time, failed; loss of eyesight; loss of savings; loss of friends; the restoration of a dissolute monarch: all this produced neither bitterness nor murmur. "Who best bear His mild yoke, they serve Him best." So he wrote and so he lived. Truly, as Macaulay says, he was weighed in the balance, and *not* found wanting.

CHRONOLOGICAL TABLE.

LITERARY.		GENERAL.	
Spenser born, ...	1552		
		The Marian Persecution,	1555
Bacon born, ...	1561		
Shakespeare born, ...	1564		
Galileo born, ...	,,	Massacre of St. Bartholomew, ...	1572
Jonson born, ...	1574		
The Faerie Queene published, ...	1590-6	The Armada, ...	1588
		Battle of Ivry, ...	1590
Shakespeare's earlier plays acted, ...	1597		
Bacon's *Essays* published,	1598	Edict of Nantes, ...	1598
		Gunpowder Plot, ...	1605
Milton born, ...	1608	Clarendon born, ...	1608
The Bible translated, ...	1611		
Shakespeare dies, ...	1616		
Milton goes to Cambridge, ...	1625	Thirty Years' War begun,	1618
		The *Mayflower* sails, ...	1620
Bunyan born, ...	1628	Laud, Bp. of London,	1628
Dryden born, ...	1631		
Milton leaves Cambridge and retires to Horton,	1632		
L'Allegro, Il Penseroso, Lycidas, &c., ...	1633-7		
Milton goes abroad, ...	1638	The Covenant signed, ...	1638
Milton settles in London,	1639	First Bishops' war, ...	1639
Newton born, ...	1642	Civil War begun, ...	1642
Areopagitica, ...	1644		

CHRONOLOGICAL TABLE—*Continued.*

Eikonoklastes,	...	...	1649	Charles I. executed, ... 1649
First Defence,	...	...	1651	
Milton becomes blind,		1652	Cromwell Protector, ... 1653
Paradise Lost begun about	1658	Cromwell dies, ... 1658
				The Restoration, ... 1660
				The Plague, ... 1665
Paradise Lost published,	1667	Clarendon's fall, ... 1667
Paradise Regained,	...	1671	France and England
Samson Agonistes,	...	1671	attack Holland, ... 1672
Milton dies,	...	...	1674	Clarendon dies, ... 1674

THE SUBJECT OF *PARADISE LOST.*

The subject of the poem as given in Book I. is the temptation and fall of man, that is, his deterioration from the state of perfect goodness and happiness, in which he was supposed to have been created, to one made up of good and evil, of happiness and unhappiness; this 'fall' being symbolised by the expulsion of Adam and Eve from Paradise or Eden. This is the central fact of the story; to it all the rest (Books I.–VIII.) is preparatory, and with it the story ends. But the preparatory events are so stupendous in their magnitude, so striking in their character, and described in such impressive language—forming, as they do, the best part of the poem—that they tend to overshadow the doings in the Garden; and so we come to look upon *Paradise Lost* as dealing rather with a series of connected events, of which the 'fall' is the first in importance but not in interest. We may, therefore, regard *Paradise Lost* as dealing with the whole universe, in its widest possible aspect; with the origin of its various parts, and their significance for man.

ANALYSIS OF THE POEM.

(A) The Fall: why and how it was brought about. I.–VIII.
(B) Its results. IX.–XII.
(C) Man's relation to the Universe and to God. Part of V.
(The third point, though not prominent, is very important in the scheme of the poem.)

(A) *The Fall: why and how it was brought about*:
  (1) Heaven; the War:
    (*a*) Its Cause, the refusal of Satan and his followers to acknowledge the Son as their head.   V.
    (*b*) The War, the expulsion of the rebels.   VI.
  (2) The Creation of the World and of Man. VII., VIII.
  (3) Hell:
    (*a*) The rebels closed in and stunned by their fall; Satan rallies his followers.   I.
    (*b*) The leaders in Council: Satan undertakes to try to ruin Man.
    (*c*) Hell and Chaos described.   } II.
    (*d*) Satan's journey through Chaos.
  (4) The World; Eden:
    (*a*) Satan explores the World.   III.
    (*b*) Adam and Eve in Eden; Satan's plottings; Raphael's warnings.   IV. and V.
    (*c*) The Fall effected.   IX.

(B) *The Results of the Fall*:
  (1) Punishment pronounced on Tempter and Tempted by the Son.   X.
  (2) Sin and Death take possession of the World, but their overthrow by the Son (*i.e.* the Redemption) is foretold.   X.
  (3) Michael reveals the future to Adam, reassures him of Redemption, and leads him and Eve out of Paradise.   XI. and XII.

(C) *Man's Relations to the Universe and to God*, as set forth by Raphael in Book V. 469–543, may be summed up briefly thus:—

"One Almighty is"; all things are created by Him, from "one first matter all"; all things are perfect in their various degrees, but are more refined and spiritual in proportion as they are near Him. In nature "the grosser feeds the purer", the soil is transformed, through the plant, into flower and fruit; the latter, used as man's nourishment, is "sublimed" into the living force which sustains the mind and the soul:

thus there is complete continuity from the lowest forms (*i.e.* mere matter) to the highest (*i.e.* pure spirit); and "all things . . . up to Him return, if not depraved from good". Raphael concludes:

> " Time may come when men
> With Angels may participate, and find
> No inconvenient diet, nor too light fare;
> And from these corporal nutriments, perhaps,
> Your bodies may at last turn all to spirit,
> Improved by tract of time, and winged ascend
> Ethereal, as we; or may at choice
> Here or in heavenly Paradises dwell,
> If ye be found obedient".

With this compare VII. 155, where the Almighty states His purpose in creating Man, viz. to replenish Heaven, lest Satan should boast of the damage inflicted: He will, He says, create

> "Of one man a race
> Of men innumerable, there to dwell,
> Not here, till, by degrees of merit raised,
> They open to themselves at length the way,
> Up hither, under long obedience tried", &c.

In this analysis the topics are arranged in chronological order. The order in the poem, as the references show, is very different, and it may be helpful to indicate it.

(1) Milton plunges into the very midst of the whole subject by depicting the rebels lying stunned on the lake after their fall: they are roused by Satan, a council is held, Man's ruin resolved on, and intrusted to Satan. Hell and Chaos are described.   I., II.

(2) Satan traverses Chaos, and explores the World, finds Eden, and plots the Fall.   II.-IV.

(3) Raphael now visits Adam and Eve. He describes their position in the universe, and warns them of their danger. In order to explain Satan's attitude, and to gratify Adam's curiosity, Raphael begins to narrate the course of events from the beginning—   V.

viz.:—the War in Heaven and the Expulsion;   VI.

and the Creation of the World.   VII.

Adam tells Raphael of his finding himself in Eden, and of the prohibition to touch the tree of knowledge.   Raphael repeats the warning, and leaves him.   VIII.

(4) They sin and are expelled.   IX.-XII.

THE COSMOLOGY OF *PARADISE LOST.*

Much of *Paradise Lost* is occupied with events that take place outside the universe as known to man—in Heaven, Hell, and Chaos; much, too, with matters connected with that universe; while the relations of the various realms to one another, and the nature of man's World as described or assumed in the poem, are so peculiar and so fundamental, that clear ideas on the subject are of the highest importance.

On reading the poem we find that Book I. does not begin the story, for there the War in Heaven is over and the rebels are undergoing punishment elsewhere; it is not till Books V.-VI. that the Angel Raphael is introduced, giving Adam a "full narration" of things from the beginning—and it is chiefly by means of these later books that we construct the key to the earlier ones.

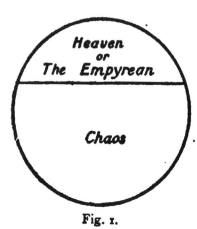

Fig. 1.

I. At the earliest period referred to by Raphael, Space consists of two parts, Heaven or the Empyrean, and Chaos:[1] "as yet this World was not", nor Man, nor Hell. Heaven alone is created, or formed: the rest of space is a blank. This stage we may symbolise[2] by figure 1. Heaven, we gather, is the region of light and life, the abode of God and the Angels—"the Sons of God".   Of its size and shape nothing definite is said.   It is totally cut off by means

---

[1] *Heaven*, perhaps that which is 'heaved' up: *Empyrean* (Gk.), 'made of fire' (the purest of the four elements); *Chaos*, the chasm, cleft, or abyss.

[2] The diagrams are merely symbolic: the form of Space, the relative magnitude of Heaven, Chaos, and Hell, and the exact position of the World are not indicated in the poem.

of a crystal floor from Chaos; various ornamental features are mentioned—as gates, battlements, and walls; and its beauty is suggested by descriptions of ideal earthly scenery, "heavenly paradises". The Angels are of two kinds—Cherubim and Seraphim, arranged in three ranks — Archangels or Chiefs, Princes, and individual Powers or Intelligences,[1] each kind having its special duties: the peculiar nature and mode of existence of these immaterial beings are described— their immortality, their might, their power of assuming any shape, and so forth. In all this Milton follows hints from the Scriptures, especially the vision of St. John (in the Book of *Revelation*), Jewish writings, Dante, and the traditions of the early and middle ages. He cautions us that his language is merely symbolical.

The Almighty, Himself invisible, has His throne on a central mount, clouded in dazzling brightness, where He receives the adoration of His sons, and makes known His commands.

Chaos,[2] "the Deep" or "the Abyss", is the name which Milton gives to that portion of space which lies outside Heaven. Its nature is inconceivable and indescribable, for it consists of that which has not yet been organised into matter,—neither earth, air, fire, nor water. The whole region is utterly devoid of life and light; it is left by the Almighty in utter confusion and darkness—"to the sway of Anarchy and Night":

"a dark
Illimitable ocean, without bound,
Without dimension: where length, breadth, and highth,
And time, and place, are lost; where eldest Night
And Chaos, ancestors of Nature, hold
Eternal anarchy, amidst the noise
Of endless wars, and by confusion stand.
For Hot, Cold, Moist, and Dry, four champions fierce,
Strive here for mastery, and to battle bring
Their embryon atoms" (II. 891-900).

[1] Masson.
[2] The fullest description of Chaos and its presiding deity is given in Book II. 890-1033.

II. This division of Space continues until the revolt of the Angels, which leads to their expulsion: the floor of Heaven opens, they are driven out through the gap, and fall through "the Abyss" for nine days. Then they come to the place which the Almighty has prepared for them out of a portion of Chaos. It lies open to receive them, closes above them, and imprisons them. This new abode of theirs is called Hell: it is situated in the part of Space remotest from Heaven, in "the bottomless pit", and is partitioned off from Chaos by walls and roof of fire. Its shape is not described, but the roof is said to be vaulted (fig. 2). Within it was indeed a place of torment, "created evil, for evil

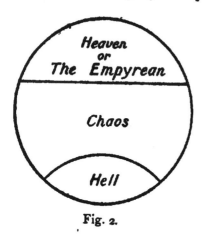

Fig. 2.

only good", "a place of fierce extremes", "with many a frozen, many a fiery Alp", "a universe of death"; so that Satan exclaims, on surveying it,

> " Here at least
> We shall be free; the Almighty hath not built
> Here for His envy, will not drive us hence ".

A means of exit into Chaos is afterwards discovered, through a gateway, guarded by two beings named Sin and Death. These open the gate for Satan, but cannot close it again: so that the Infernals can henceforth pass out and in at will.

III. After their fall the Angels lie stunned and bewildered on a burning lake for nine days, and it is during this period that the next change is brought about. For some time the Almighty had purposed creating a new World, and placing in it a new and favoured race. At His command the Messiah now issues forth "far into Chaos", and with "the golden compass" "circumscribes this Universe" of Earth, and Planets, and all that is cognisable by man. This new World hangs from the floor of Heaven by a golden chain attached to its topmost point, or zenith; but whether it is suspended from the centre of the Empyrean, and poised about the centre of Space (as suggested in diagram 3), and what its relative size, cannot be determined.[1]

Man is thus in a middle position, the Good above, the Evil below, and he is to be connected with both. For the use of the good angels a golden stairway is let down from Heaven, and for the use of the evil ones a broad path, or bridge, is made by Sin and Death through the Deep in the track taken by Satan on his journey of exploration (II. 1024, &c.).

Fig. 3.

The golden stair can be drawn up as if to secure Heaven against unwished-for visitants, but the lower bridge is never closed. The two roads meet at the same point, where there is an opening affording access to the interior of the World.

IV. Let us now look at this new World. It was created primarily[2] for a new race of beings, Man, and his abode, the Earth, is appropriately made its centre. It is a complicated system of ten hollow spheres or shells fitted one within another, and around the solid Earth. Each sphere has a motion of its own, imparted, in the first place, by the outside shell, called the Primum Mobile, or First Moved—how it is moved we are not told. Of these spheres only two are material—the Primum Mobile or hard, external casing, and the next within it, the Crystalline Sphere, which consists of a clear, watery fluid. The first is designed as a protection to the whole system, the latter to moderate the extremes of heat and cold which may permeate the outer framework. The

---

[1] Professor Masson makes the radius of the World one-third of *a* to *d*, and consequently the World stretches from *a* to *e*. This seems to agree with I. 73, 74, but not with II. 1052-3, in which the World appears to Satan in the distance "as a star of smallest magnitude", nor with III. 427-8, where the World "from the wall of Heaven, though distant far, some small reflection gains". The force of the passage (I. 73-4) depends on the meaning of the term "pole", which is rather vague, and in VII. 23, seems applicable to the point *a*.

[2] Cp. VIII. 98-9.

remaining eight are, or may be regarded as, mere divisions of space, in which the several planets or orbs have their respective orbits. It was in all probability to account for the different motions of the several planets that the separate revolutions of the spheres were assumed. The seven planetary spheres, beginning with that nearest the Earth, are:

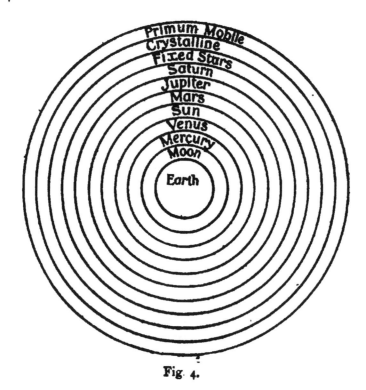

Fig. 4.

the Moon, Mercury, Venus, the Sun, Mars, Jupiter, Saturn. The eighth sphere contains those stars which occupy a fixed position with regard to one another, and it is therefore called the Fixed or the Firmament: it revolves once daily, carrying all its stars round with it. The Earth is supposed to be stationary.

This theory of the World was gradually given up in favour of the simpler one of Copernicus (1473-1543), which was advocated by Galileo and others, and finally established by Kepler and Newton. According to this the Sun is the centre[1]

---

[1] More correctly, the sun is not at the centre, but at the common focus of the ellipses of the paths described by the planets.

of our universe, and is almost stationary; the Earth and the other planets revolve about it, whilst some of these planets, e.g. the Earth, have satellites of their own; and finally the 'fixed stars' are outside the solar universe altogether.

Milton was well acquainted with the Copernican system, and may quite possibly have accepted it; but in a poem concerned with topics so far beyond the pale of experience and knowledge, and so full of ancient and mediæval ideas, beliefs, and fancies, the old theory, however erroneous, was not only fitting, but necessary; for it is involved in very many of the thoughts borrowed by Milton, as it is in some of our phrases at this day;[1] in Milton's time it was still generally accepted, and it was undoubtedly more poetical than the new system.[2]

THE METRE.

(1) The poem is written in blank verse, or unrimed iambic pentameters; that is, the typical line consists of ten syllables, divided into five feet of two syllables each, the stress falling on the second syllable, e.g.—

With gems' | and gold' | en lus' | tre rich' | embla'zed.

(2) A repetition of such typical lines, even if possible, would be extremely wearisome; and we find the lines modified in various ways:

(a) by an additional syllable at the end of the line; e.g. I. 38;

---

[1] Professor Masson instances such phrases as 'out of one's sphere'.

[2] Consider e.g. the quaint fancy of the music of the spheres as expressed by Shakespeare (Merchant of Venice, V. i. 60)—

> "There's not the smallest orb which thou behold'st
> But in his motion like an angel sings,
> Still quiring to the young-eyed cherubins;
> Such harmony is in immortal souls;
> But, whilst this muddy vesture of decay
> Doth grossly close it in, we cannot hear it."

(*b*) by additional syllables not at the end; such syllables are usually elided: *e.g.*—

> Above' | the *Ā* on' | *ĭăn* mount', | while it' | pursues'.
>
> His tem' | ple right' | against' ¦ the tem' | ple of God'.

The *e* of passive participles in -*ed* and -*en* is usually elided.

(*c*) one or even two of the five stresses may be dropped: *e.g.*—

> Ā dun' | geon hor' | rible on all' | sides round',

where the stress fails in the third foot owing to the syllable -*ble*.

(*d*) or the stress may be inverted: *e.g.*—

> Herd for | his en' | vy; will' | not drive' | us' hence.
>
> Ā mind' | not' to | be changed' | by place' | or time'.

(The inverted feet are *trochees*.)

(3) The *breaks* in the sentences do not come at the ends of the lines only; but the construction is carried on without regard to the division into lines, and we get longer or shorter groups just as the case requires. Thus, the end of a sentence may occur in any part of the line or at the end. This gives ten possible positions, but there are frequently two breaks in one line. The result is such variety in the groupings, and such a fitness between thought and language, that there is never even an approach to monotony.

PARADISE LOST.

BOOK I.

The subject of the poem, Man's fall.   Invocation of the Holy Spirit's
aid.

OF Man's first disobedience, and the fruit
Of that forbidden tree, whose mortal taste
Brought death into the World, and all our woe,
With loss of Eden, till one greater Man
Restore us, and regain the blissful seat,   5
Sing, Heavenly Muse, that on the secret top
Of Oreb, or of Sinai, didst inspire
That shepherd who first taught the chosen seed
In the beginning how the Heavens and Earth
Rose out of Chaos: or, if Sion hill   10
Delight thee more, and Siloa's brook that flow'd
Fast by the oracle of God, I thence
Invoke thy aid to my adventurous song,
That with no middle flight intends to soar
Above the Aonian mount, while it pursues   15
Things unattempted yet in prose or rhime.
And chiefly thou, O Spirit, that dost prefer
Before all temples the upright heart and pure,
Instruct me, for thou know'st; thou from the first
Wast present, and, with mighty wings outspread,   20
Dove-like sat'st brooding on the vast Abyss,
And mad'st it pregnant: what in me is dark
Illumine, what is low raise and support;
That to the highth of this great argument

I may assert Eternal Providence,   25
And justify the ways of God to men.

*Man's fall caused by Satan in revenge for his expulsion from
Heaven.*

Say first—for Heaven hides nothing from thy view,
Nor the deep tract of hell—say first what cause
Moved our grand parents, in that happy state,
Favoured of Heaven so highly, to fall off   30
From their Creator, and transgress his will
For one restraint, lords of the World besides.
Who first seduced them to that foul revolt?
The infernal Serpent; he it was, whose guile,
Stirred up with envy and revenge, deceived   35
The mother of mankind, what time his pride
Had cast him out from Heaven, with all his host
Of rebel Angels, by whose aid, aspiring
To set himself in glory above his peers,
He trusted to have equalled the Most High,   40
If he opposed; and with ambitious aim
Against the throne and monarchy of God
Raised impious war in Heaven and battle proud,
With vain attempt.   Him the Almighty Power
Hurled headlong flaming from the ethereal sky,   45
With hideous ruin and combustion, down
To bottomless perdition, there to dwell
In adamantine chains and penal fire,
Who durst defy the Omnipotent to arms.

*Satan, recovering from his stupor, "views the situation": Hell
described.*

Nine times the space that measures day and night   50
To mortal men, he, with his horrid crew,
Lay vanquished, rolling in the fiery gulf,
Confounded, though immortal.   But his doom
Reserved him to more wrath; for now the thought

Both of lost happiness and lasting pain 55
Torments him; round he throws his baleful eyes,
That witnessed huge affliction and dismay,
Mixed with obdúrate pride and steadfast hate.
At once, as far as Angel's ken, he views
The dismal situation, waste and wild. 60
A dungeon horrible, on all sides round,
As one great furnace flamed; yet from those flames
No light; but rather darkness visible
Served only to discover sights of woe,
Regions of sorrow, doleful shades, where peace 65
And rest can never dwell, hope never comes
That comes to all, but torture without end
Still urges, and a fiery deluge, fed
With ever-burning sulphur unconsumed.
Such place Eternal Justice had prepared 70
For those rebellious; here their prison ordained
In utter darkness, and their portion set,
As far removed from God and light of Heaven,
As from the centre thrice to the utmost pole.
Oh, how unlike the place from whence they fell! 75
There the companions of his fall, o'erwhelmed
With floods and whirlwinds of tempestuous fire,
He soon discerns; and, weltering by his side,
One next himself in power, and next in crime,
Long after known in Palestine, and named 80
Beëlzebub. To whom the Arch-Enemy,
And thence in Heaven called Satan, with bold words
Breaking the horrid silence, thus began:—

Satan's speech to his comrade Beëlzebub: he avows undying hate,
and urges " eternal war".

"If thou beest he—but Oh, how fallen! how changed
From him!—who, in the happy realms of light, 85

Clothed with transcendent brightness, didst outshine
Myriads, though bright—if he whom mutual league,
United thoughts and counsels, equal hope
And hazard in the glorious enterprise,
Joined with me once, now misery hath joined   90
In equal ruin; into what pit thou seest
From what highth fallen: so much the stronger proved
He with his thunder: and till then who knew
The force of those dire arms?   Yet not for those,
Nor what the potent Victor in his rage   95
Can else inflict, do I repent, or change,
Though changed in outward lustre, that fixed mind,
And high disdain from sense of injured merit,
That with the Mightiest raised me to contend,
And to the fierce contention brought along   100
Innumerable force of Spirits armed,
That durst dislike his reign, and, me preferring,
His utmost power with adverse power opposed
In dubious battle on the plains of Heaven,   104
And shook his throne.   What though the field be lost?
All is not lost—the unconquerable will,
And study of revenge, immortal hate,
And courage never to submit or yield:
And what is else not to be overcome.
That glory never shall his wrath or might   110
Extort from me.   To bow and sue for grace
With suppliant knee, and deify his power
Who, from the terror of this arm, so late
Doubted his empire—that were low indeed;
That were an ignominy and shame beneath   115
This downfall; since, by fate, the strength of gods,
And this empyreal substance, cannot fail;
Since, through experience of this great event,
In arms not worse, in foresight much advanced,

We may with more successful hope resolve   120
To wage by force or guile eternal war,
Irreconcilable to our grand foe,
Who now triumphs, and in the excess of joy
Sole reigning holds the tyranny of Heaven."
    So spake the apostate Angel, though in pain,   125
Vaunting aloud, but racked with deep despair;
And him thus answered soon his bold compeer:—

Beëlzebub's reply: he is less hopeful:—' What avails it if we live only to suffer ?'

"O Prince, O Chief of many thronèd powers
That led the embattled Seraphim to war
Under thy conduct, and, in dreadful deeds   130
Fearless, endangered Heaven's perpetual King,
And put to proof his high supremacy,
Whether upheld by strength, or chance, or fate!
Too well I see and rue the dire event
That, with sad overthrow and foul defeat,   135
Hath lost us Heaven, and all this mighty host
In horrible destruction laid thus low,
As far as gods and Heavenly essences
Can perish: for the mind and spirit remains
Invincible, and vigour soon returns,   140
Though all our glory extinct, and happy state
. Here swallowed up in endless misery.
But what if he our conqueror (whom I now
Of force believe almighty, since no less
Than such could have o'erpowered such force as ours)
Have left us this our spirit and strength entire,   146
Strongly to suffer and support our pains,
That we may so suffice his vengeful ire,
Or do him mightier service as his thralls
By right of war, whate'er his business be,   150

Here in the heart of Hell to work in fire,
Or do his errands in the gloomy Deep?
What can it then avail though yet we feel
Strength undiminished, or eternal being
To undergo eternal punishment?"   155
Whereto with speedy words the Arch-Fiend replied:—

Satan's rejoinder: ' Revenge is sweet; we can live to thwart our
enemy.'

"Fallen Cherub, to be weak is miserable,
Doing or suffering: but of this be sure—
To do aught good never will be our task,
But ever to do ill our sole delight,   160
As being the contrary to his high will
Whom we resist.   If then his providence
Out of our evil seek to bring forth good,
Our labour must be to pervert that end,
And out of good still to find means of evil;   165
Which ofttimes may succeed so as perhaps
Shall grieve him, if I fail not, and disturb
His inmost counsels from their destined aim.

' The storm is over: let us muster our forces and consult together.'

But see! the angry victor hath recalled
His ministers of vengeance and pursuit   170
Back to the gates of Heaven: the sulphurous hail,
Shot after us in storm, o'erblown hath laid
The fiery surge that from the precipice
Of Heaven received us falling; and the thunder,
Winged with red lightning and impetuous rage,   175
Perhaps hath spent his shafts, and ceases now
To bellow through the vast and boundless Deep.
Let us not slip the occasion, whether scorn
Or satiate fury yield it from our foe.
Seest thou yon dreary plain, forlorn and wild,   180

The seat of desolation, void of light,
Save what the glimmering of these livid flames
Casts pale and dreadful?   Thither let us tend
From off the tossing of these fiery waves;
There rest, if any rest can harbour there;   185
And, reassembling our afflicted powers,
Consult how we may henceforth most offend
Our enemy, our own loss how repair,
How overcome this dire calamity,
What reinforcement we may gain from hope,   190
If not, what resolution from despair."

Satan's vastness suggested by comparisons.

Thus Satan, talking to his nearest mate,
With head uplift above the wave, and eyes
That sparkling blazed; his other parts besides
Prone on the flood, extended long and large,   195
Lay floating many a rood, in bulk as huge
As whom the fables name of monstrous size,
Titanian or Earth-born, that warred on Jove,
Briareos or Typhon, whom the den
By ancient Tarsus held, or that sea-beast   200
Leviathan, which God of all his works
Created hugest that swim the ocean stream.
Him, haply slumbering on the Norway foam,
The pilot of some small night-foundered skiff,
Deeming some island, oft, as seamen tell,   205
With fixed anchor in his scaly rind,
Moors by his side under the lee, while night
Invests the sea, and wishèd morn delays.

He is allowed to rise.

So stretched out huge in length the Arch-Fiend lay,
Chained on the burning lake; nor ever thence   210

Had risen, or heaved his head, but that the will
And high permission of all-ruling Heaven
Left him at large to his own dark designs,
That with reiterated crimes he might
Heap on himself damnation, while he sought   215
Evil to others, and enraged might see
How all his malice served but to bring forth
Infinite goodness, grace, and mercy, shown
On Man by him seduced, but on himself
Treble confusion, wrath, and vengeance poured.   220

Satan and Beëlzebub fly to land: the land described.

Forthwith upright he rears from off the pool
His mighty stature; on each hand the flames
Driven backward slope their pointing spires, and, rolled
In billows, leave in the midst a horrid vale.
Then with expanded wings he steers his flight   225
Aloft, incumbent on the dusky air,
That felt unusual weight; till on dry land
He lights—if it were land that ever burned
With solid, as the lake with liquid fire,
And such appeared in hue as when the force   230
Of subterranean wind transports a hill
Torn from Pelorus, or the shattered side
Of thundering Ætna, whose combustible
And fueled entrails, thence conceiving fire,
Sublimed with mineral fury, aid the winds,   235
And leave a singed bottom all involved
With stench and smoke.   Such resting found the sole
Of unblest feet.   Him followed his next mate;
Both glorying to have scaped the Stygian flood
As gods, and by their own recovered strength,   240
Not by the sufferance of supernal power.

Satan's soliloquy on viewing their new abode.

"Is this the region, this the soil, the clime,"
Said then the lost Archangel, "this the seat
That we must change for Heaven? this mournful gloom
For that celestial light?   Be it so, since he   245
Who now is sovran can dispose and bid
What shall be right: farthest from him is best,
Whom reason hath equalled, force hath made supreme
Above his equals.   Farewell, happy fields,
Where joy for ever dwells!   Hail, horrors! hail,   250
Infernal world! and thou, profoundest Hell,
Receive thy new possessor—one who brings
A mind not to be changed by place or time.
The mind is its own place, and in itself
Can make a Heaven of Hell, a Hell of Heaven.   255
What matter where, if I be still the same,
And what I should be, all but less than he
Whom thunder hath made greater?   Here at least
We shall be free; the Almighty hath not built
Here for his envy, will not drive us hence: 260
Here we may reign secure; and, in my choice,
To reign is worth ambition, though in Hell:
Better to reign in Hell than serve in Heaven.

They agree to rouse and rally their followers.

But wherefore let we then our faithful friends,
The associates and co-partners of our loss,   265
Lie thus astonished on the oblivious pool,
And call them not to share with us their part
In this unhappy mansion, or once more
With rallied arms to try what may be yet
Regained in Heaven, or what more lost in Hell?"   270
    So Satan spake; and him Beëlzebub
Thus answered:—"Leader of those armies bright
    (M 46)   C

Which, but the Omnipotent, none could have foiled!
If once they hear that voice, their liveliest pledge
Of hope in fears and dangers—heard so oft   275
In worst extremes, and on the perilous edge
Of battle, when it raged, in all assaults
Their surest signal—they will soon resume
New courage, and revive, though now they lie
Grovelling and prostrate on yon lake of fire,   80
As we erewhile, astounded and amazed;
No wonder, fallen such a pernicious highth!"

The appearance of Satan as he makes for the shore, and of his
legions as they lie on the lake.

He scarce had ceased when the superior Fiend
Was moving toward the shore; his ponderous shield,
Ethereal temper, massy, large, and round,   285
Behind him cast.   The broad circumference
Hung on his shoulders like the moon, whose orb
Through optic glass the Tuscan artist views
At evening, from the top of Fesolé,
Or in Valdarno, to descry new lands,   290
Rivers, or mountains, in her spotty globe.
His spear—to equal which the tallest pine
Hewn on Norwegian hills, to be the mast
Of some great ammiral, were but a wand—
He walked with, to support uneasy steps   295
Over the burning marle, not like those steps
On Heaven's azure; and the torrid clime
Smote on him sore besides, vaulted with fire.
Nathless he so endured, till on the beach
Of that inflamed sea he stood, and called   300
His legions—Angel forms, who lay entranced,
Thick as autumnal leaves that strew the brooks
In Vallombrosa, where the Etrurian shades

High over-arched imbower; or scattered sedge
Afloat, when with fierce winds Orion armed   305
Hath vexed the Red-Sea coast, whose waves o'erthrew
Busiris and his Memphian chivalry,
While with perfidious hatred they pursued
The sojourners of Goshen, who beheld
From the safe shore their floating carcases   310
And broken chariot-wheels.   So thick bestrewn,
Abject and lost, lay these, covering the flood,
Under amazement of their hideous change.

Satan taunts them for their inactivity, and calls them to arms.

He called so loud, that all the hollow deep
Of Hell resounded: "Princes, Potentates,   .   315
Warriors, the flower of Heaven—once yours; now lost,
If such astonishment as this can seize
Eternal Spirits!   Or have ye chosen this place
After the toil of battle to repose
Your wearied virtue, for the ease you find   320
To slumber here, as in the vales of Heaven?
Or in this abject posture have ye sworn
To adore the conqueror, who now beholds
Cherub and Seraph rolling in the flood
With scattered arms and ensigns, till anon   325
His swift pursuers from Heaven-gates discern
The advantage, and, descending, tread us down
Thus drooping, or with linked thunderbolts
Transfix us to the bottom of this gulf?—
Awake, arise, or be for ever fallen!"   330

Their appearance: their multitude suggested by comparisons.

They heard, and were abashed, and up they sprung
Upon the wing, as when men wont to watch,
On duty sleeping found by whom they dread,

Rouse and bestir themselves ere well awake.
Nor did they not perceive the evil plight   335
In which they were, or the fierce pains not feel;
Yet to their General's voice they soon obeyed
Innumerable.   As when the potent rod
Of Amram's son, in Egypt's evil day,
Waved round the coast, up-called a pitchy cloud   340
Of locusts, warping on the eastern wind,
That o'er the realm of impious Pharaoh hung
Like night, and darkened all the land of Nile;
So numberless were those bad Angels seen
Hovering on wing under the cope of Hell,   345
'Twixt upper, nether, and surrounding fires;
Till, as a signal given, the uplifted spear
Of their great Sultan waving to direct
Their course, in even balance down they light
On the firm brimstone, and fill all the plain: 350
A multitude like which the populous North
Poured never from her frozen loins to pass
Rhene or the Danaw, when her barbarous sons
Came like a deluge on the South, and spread
Beneath Gibraltar to the Libyan sands.   355

The leaders come forward—for the time being, nameless.

Forthwith, from every squadron and each band,
The heads and leaders thither haste where stood
Their great Commander—godlike shapes, and forms
Excelling human; princely dignities;
And powers that erst in Heaven sat on thrones,   360
Though of their names in Heavenly records now
Be no memorial, blotted out and rased
By their rebellion from the Books of Life.
Nor had they yet among the sons of Eve
Got them new names, till, wandering o'er the Earth, 365

Through God's high sufferance for the trial of Man,
By falsities and lies the greatest part
Of Mankind they corrupted to forsake
God their Creator, and the invisible
Glory of him that made them to transform   370
Oft to the image of a brute, adorned
With gay religions full of pomp and gold,
And devils to adore for deities:
Then were they known to men by various names,
And various idols through the heathen world.   375

The leaders enumerated and described under the names they
afterwards acquired as heathen deities.

Say, Muse, their names then known, who first, who last,
Roused from the slumber on that fiery couch,
At their great Emperor's call, as next in worth
Came singly where he stood on the bare strand,
While the promiscuous crowd stood yet aloof.   380
The chief were those who, from the pit of Hell
Roaming to seek their prey on Earth, durst fix
Their seats, long after, next the seat of God,
Their altars by his altar, gods adored
Among the nations round, and durst abide   385
Jehovah thundering out of Sion, throned
Between the Cherubim; yea, often placed
Within his sanctuary itself their shrines,
Abominations; and with cursed things
His holy rites and solemn feasts profaned,   390
And with their darkness durst affront his light.
First, Moloch, horrid king, besmeared with blood
Of human sacrifice, and parents' tears;
Though, for the noise of drums and timbrels loud,
Their children's cries unheard that passed through fire
To his grim idol.   Him the Ammonite   396

Worshipped in Rabba and her watery plain,
In Argob and in Bashan, to the stream
Of utmost Arnon.   Nor content with such
Audacious neighbourhood, the wisest heart   400
Of Solomon he led by fraud to build
His temple right against the temple of God,
On that opprobrious hill, and made his grove
The pleasant valley of Hinnom, Tophet thence
And black Gehenna called, the type of Hell.   405
Next Chemos, the obscene dread of Moab's sons,
From Aroer to Nebo and the wild
Of southmost Abarim; in Hesebon
And Horonaim, Seon's realm, beyond
The flowery dale of Sibma clad with vines,   410
And Eleäle to the Asphaltic pool:
Peor his other name, when he enticed
Israel in Sittim, on their march from Nile,
To do him wanton rites, which cost them woe.
Yet thence his lustful orgies he enlarged   415
Even to that hill of scandal, by the grove
Of Moloch homicide, lust hard by hate;
Till good Josiah drove them thence to Hell.
With these came they who, from the bordering flood
Of old Euphrates to the brook that parts   420
Egypt from Syrian ground, had general names
Of Baälim and Ashtaroth—those male,
These feminine.   For Spirits, when they please,
Can either sex assume, or both; so soft
And uncompounded is their essence pure,   425
Not tied or manacled with joint or limb,
Nor founded on the brittle strength of bones,
Like cumbrous flesh; but in what shape they choose,
Dilated or condensed, bright or obscure,
Can execute their aery purposes,   430

And works of love or enmity fulfil.
For those the race of Israel oft forsook
Their living Strength, and unfrequented left
His righteous altar, bowing lowly down
To bestial gods; for which their heads, as low   435
Bowed down in battle, sunk before the spear
Of despicable foes.   With these in troop
Came Ashtoreth, whom the Phœnicians called
Astarte, Queen of Heaven, with crescent horns;
To whose bright image nightly by the moon   440
Sidonian virgins paid their vows and songs;
In Sion also not unsung, where stood
Her temple on the offensive mountain, built
By that uxorious king whose heart, though large,
Beguiled by fair idolatresses, fell   445
To idols foul.   Thammuz came next behind,
Whose annual wound in Lebanon allured
The Syrian damsels to lament his fate
In amorous ditties all a summer's day,
While smooth Adonis from his native rock   450
Ran purple to the sea, supposed with blood
Of Thammuz yearly wounded: the love-tale
Infected Sion's daughters with like heat,
Whose wanton passions in the sacred porch
Ezekiel saw, when, by the vision led,   455
His eye surveyed the dark idolatries
Of alienated Judah.   Next came one
Who mourned in earnest, when the captive ark
Maimed his brute image, head and hands lopt off,
In his own temple, on the grunsel-edge,   460
Where he fell flat and shamed his worshippers:
Dagon his name, sea-monster, upward man
And downward fish; yet had his temple high
Reared in Azotus, dreaded through the coast

Of Palestine, in Gath and Ascalon,   465
And Accaron and Gaza's frontier bounds.
Him followed Rimmon, whose delightful seat
Was fair Damascus, on the fertile banks
Of Abana and Pharphar, lucid streams.
He also against the house of God was bold: 470
A leper once he lost, and gained a king—
Ahaz, his sottish conqueror, whom he drew
God's altar to disparage and displace
For one of Syrian mode, whereon to burn
His odious offerings, and adore the gods   475
Whom he had vanquished.   After these appeared
A crew who, under names of old renown—
Osiris, Isis, Orus, and their train—
With monstrous shapes and sorceries abused
Fanatic Egypt and her priests to seek   480
Their wandering gods disguised in brutish forms
Rather than human.   Nor did Israel scape
The infection, when their borrowed gold composed
The calf in Oreb; and the rebel king
Doubled that sin in Bethel and in Dan,   485
Likening his Maker to the grazed ox—   .
Jehovah, who, in one night, when he passed
From Egypt marching, equalled with one stroke
Both her first-born and all her bleating gods.
Belial came last; than whom a Spirit more lewd   490
Fell not from Heaven, or more gross to love
Vice for itself.   To him no temple stood
Or altar smoked; yet who more oft than he
In temples and at altars, when the priest
Turns atheist, as did Eli's sons, who filled   495
With lust and violence the house of God?
In courts and palaces he also reigns,
And in luxurious cities, where the noise

Of riot ascends above their loftiest towers,
And injury and outrage; and, when night 500
Darkens the streets, then wander forth the sons
Of Belial, flown with insolence and wine.
Witness the streets of Sodom, and that night
In Gibeah, when the hospitable door
Exposed a matron, to avoid worse rape. 505
These were the prime in order and in might:
The rest were long to tell; though far renowned,
The Ionian gods of Javan's issue held
Gods, yet confessed later than Heaven and Earth,
Their boasted parents;—Titan, Heaven's first-born, 510
With his enormous brood, and birthright seized
By younger Saturn: he from mightier Jove,
His own and Rhea's son, like measure found;
So Jove usurping reigned. These, first in Crete
And Ida known, thence on the snowy top 515
Of cold Olympus ruled the middle air,
Their highest Heaven; or on the Delphian cliff,
Or in Dodona, and through all the bounds
Of Doric land; or who with Saturn old
Fled over Adria to the Hesperian fields, 520
And o'er the Celtic roamed the utmost isles.

The leaders having assembled, Satan cheers them and bids Azazel
raise the standard

All these and more came flocking; but with looks
Downcast and damp; yet such wherein appeared
Obscure some glimpse of joy to have found their Chief
Not in despair, to have found themselves not lost 525
In loss itself; which on his countenance cast
Like doubtful hue. But he, his wonted pride
Soon recollecting, with high words, that bore
Semblance of worth, not substance, gently raised

Their fainting courage, and dispelled their fears: 530
Then straight commands that, at the warlike sound
Of trumpets loud and clarions, be upreared
His mighty standard.   That proud honour claimed
Azazel as his right, a Cherub tall:
Who forthwith from the glittering staff unfurled 535
The imperial ensign; which, full high advanced,
Shone like a meteor streaming to the wind,
With gems and golden lustre rich imblazed,
Seraphic arms and trophies; all the while
Sonorous metal blowing martial sounds: 540
At which the universal host up-sent
A shout that tore Hell's concave, and beyond
Frighted the reign of Chaos and old Night.

*Thereupon their followers form in battle array and march to
Dorian music.*

All in a moment through the gloom were seen
Ten thousand banners rise into the air, 545
With orient colours waving: with them rose
A forest huge of spears; and thronging helms
Appeared, and serried shields in thick array
Of depth immeasurable.   Anon they move
In perfect phalanx to the Dorian mood 550
Of flutes and soft recorders—such as raised
To highth of noblest temper heroes old
Arming to battle, and instead of rage
Deliberate valour breathed, firm, and unmoved
With dread of death to flight or foul retreat; 555
Nor wanting power to mitigate and swage
With solemn touches troubled thoughts, and chase
Anguish and doubt and fear and sorrow and pain
From mortal or immortal minds.   Thus they,
Breathing united force with fixèd thought, 560

Moved on in silence to soft pipes that charmed
Their painful steps o'er the burnt soil.   And now

Satan views his army, compared with which the greatest forces of
ancient or mediæval times are insignificant.

Advanced in view they stand—a horrid front
Of dreadful length and dazzling arms, in guise
Of warriors old, with ordered spear and shield,   565
Awaiting what command their mighty Chief
Had to impose.   He through the armèd files
Darts his experienced eye, and soon traverse
The whole battalion views—their order due,
Their visages and stature as of gods;   570
Their number last he sums.   And now his heart
Distends with pride, and, hardening in his strength,
Glories: for never, since created Man,
Met such embodied force as, named with these,
Could merit more than that small infantry   575
Warred on by cranes—though all the giant brood
Of Phlegra with the heroic race were joined
That fought at Thebes and Ilium, on each side
Mixed with auxiliar gods; and what resounds
In fable or romance of Uther's son,   580
Begirt with British and Armoric knights;
And all who since, baptized or infidel,
Jousted in Aspramont or Montalban,
Damasco, or Marocco, or Trebisond,
Or whom Biserta sent from Afric shore,   585
When Charlemain with all his peerage fell
By Fontarabbia.   Thus far these beyond
Compare of mortal prowess, yet observed

The appearance of Satan and his host suggested by various
similes.

Their dread Commander.   He, above the rest
In shape and gesture proudly eminent,   590

Stood like a tower.   His form had yet not lost
All her original brightness, nor appeared
Less than archangel ruined, and the excess
Of glory obscured: as when the sun new-risen
Looks through the horizontal misty air   595
Shorn of his beams, or, from behind the moon,
In dim eclipse, disastrous twilight sheds
On half the nations, and with fear of change
Perplexes monarchs.   Darkened so, yet shone
Above them all the Archangel: but his face   600
Deep scars of thunder had intrenched, and care
Sat on his faded cheek, but under brows
Of dauntless courage, and considerate pride
Waiting revenge.   Cruel his eye, but cast
Signs of remorse and passion, to behold   605
The fellows of his crime, the followers rather
(Far other once beheld in bliss), condemned
For ever now to have their lot in pain—
Millions of Spirits for his fault amerced
Of Heaven, and from eternal splendours flung   610
For his revolt—yet faithful how they stood,
Their glory withered; as, when Heaven's fire
Hath scathed the forest oaks or mountain pines,
With singed top their stately growth, though bare,
Stands on the blasted heath.   He now prepared   615
To speak; whereat their doubled ranks they bend
From wing to wing, and half enclose him round
With all his peers: attention held them mute.
Thrice he assayed, and thrice, in spite of scorn,
Tears, such as Angels weep, burst forth: at last   620
Words interwove with sighs found out their way:—

Satan harangues his host: 'their defeat was due to ignorance of the enemy's strength.'

"O myriads of immortal Spirits!   O Powers
Matchless, but with the Almighty!—and that strife
Was not inglorious, though the event was dire,
As this place testifies, and this dire change   625
Hateful to utter.   But what power of mind,
Foreseeing or presaging from the depth
Of knowledge past or present, could have feared,
How such united force of gods, how such
As stood like these, could ever know repulse?   630
For who can yet believe, though after loss,
That all these puissant legions, whose exile
Hath emptied Heaven, shall fail to reascend,
Self-raised, and repossess their native seat?
For me, be witness all the host of Heaven,   635
If counsels different, or dangers shunned
By me, have lost our hopes.   But he who reigns
Monarch in Heaven till then as one secure
Sat on his throne, upheld by old repute,
Consent or custom, and his regal state   640
Put forth at full, but still his strength concealed—
Which tempted our attempt, and wrought our fall.

Henceforth they must oppose him by guile; a visit to the new-formed world suggested; war resolved on.

Henceforth his might we know, and know our own,
So as not either to provoke, or dread
New war provoked: our better part remains   645
To work in close design, by fraud or guile,
What force effected not; that he no less
At length from us may find, who overcomes
By force hath overcome but half his foe.
Space may produce new worlds; whereof so rife   650

There went a fame in Heaven that he ere long
Intended to create, and therein plant
A generation whom his choice regard
Should favour equal to the Sons of Heaven.
Thither, if but to pry, shall be perhaps   655
Our first eruption—thither, or elsewhere;
For this infernal pit shall never hold
Celestial Spirits in bondage, nor the Abyss
Long under darkness cover.   But these thoughts
Full counsel must mature.   Peace is despaired;   660
For who can think submission?   War, then, war
Open or understood, must be resolved."
He spake; and, to confirm his words, out-flew
Millions of flaming swords, drawn from the thighs
Of mighty Cherubim; the sudden blaze   665
Far round illumined Hell.   Highly they raged
Against the Highest, and fierce with graspèd arms
Clashed on their sounding shields the din of war
Hurling defiance toward the vault of Heaven.

*Led by Mammon they quarry gold and cast it, ready for use in
building their palace.*

There stood a hill not far, whose grisly top   670
Belched fire and rolling smoke; the rest entire
Shone with a glossy scurf—undoubted sign
That in his womb was hid metallic ore,
The work of sulphur.   Thither, winged with speed,
A numerous brigad hastened: as when bands   675
Of pioners, with spade and pickaxe armed,
Forerun the royal camp, to trench a field,
Or cast a rampart.   Mammon led them on—
Mammon, the least erected Spirit that fell   679
From Heaven; for even in Heaven his looks and thoughts
Were always downward bent, admiring more

The riches of Heaven's pavement, trodden gold,
Than aught divine or holy else enjoyed
In vision beatific.   By him first
Men also, and by his suggestion taught,   685
Ransacked the centre, and with impious hands
Rifled the bowels of their mother Earth
For treasures better hid.   Soon had his crew
Opened into the hill a spacious wound,
And digged out ribs of gold.   Let none admire 690
That riches grow in Hell; that soil may best
Deserve the precious bane.   And here let those
Who boast in mortal things, and wondering tell
Of Babel, and the works of Memphian kings,
Learn how their greatest monuments of fame,   695
And strength, and art, are easily outdone
By Spirits reprobate, and in an hour
What in an age they, with incessant toil
And hands innumerable, scarce perform.
Nigh on the plain, in many cells prepared,   700
That underneath had veins of liquid fire
Sluiced from the lake, a second multitude
With wondrous art founded the massy ore,
Severing each kind, and scummed the bullion-dross.
A third as soon had formed within the ground   705
A various mould, and from the boiling cells
By strange conveyance filled each hollow nook;
As in an organ, from one blast of wind,
To many a row of pipes the sound-board breathes.

Pandemonium described: its architect, Mulciber.

Anon out of the earth a fabric huge   710
Rose, like an exhalation, with the sound
Of dulcet symphonies and voices sweet—
Built like a temple, where pilasters round

Were set, and Doric pillars overlaid
With golden architrave; nor did there want   715
Cornice or frieze with bossy sculptures graven:
The roof was fretted gold.   Not Babylon
Nor great Alcairo such magnificence
Equalled in all their glories, to enshrine
Belus or Serapis their gods, or seat   720
Their kings, when Egypt with Assyria strove
In wealth and luxury.   The ascending pile
Stood fixed her stately highth; and straight the doors,
Opening their brazen folds, discover, wide
Within, her ample spaces o'er the smooth   725
And level pavement: from the archèd roof,
Pendent by subtle magic, many a row
Of starry lamps and blazing cressets, fed
With naphtha and asphaltus, yielded light
As from a sky.   The hasty multitude   730
Admiring entered; and the work some praise,
And some the architect.   His hand was known
In Heaven by many a towered structure high,
Where sceptred Angels held their residence,
And sat as princes, whom the supreme King   735
Exalted to such power, and gave to rule,
Each in his Hierarchy, the Orders bright.
Nor was his name unheard or unadored
In ancient Greece; and in Ausonian land
Men called him Mulciber; and how he fell   740
From Heaven they fabled, thrown by angry Jove
Sheer o'er the crystal battlements: from morn
To noon he fell, from noon to dewy eve,
A summer's day, and with the setting sun
Dropped from the zenith, like a falling star,   745
On Lemnos, the Ægean isle.   Thus they relate,
Erring; for he with this rebellious rout

Fell long before; nor aught availed him now
To have built in Heaven high towers; nor did he scape
By all his engines, but was headlong sent,   750
With his industrious crew, to build in Hell.

" The worthiest" summoned to a council, they and their attend-
ants swarm in, and fill the hall " both on the ground and in
the air".

Meanwhile the wingèd heralds, by command
Of sovran power, with awful ceremony
And trumpet's sound, throughout the host proclaim
A solemn council forthwith to be held   755
At Pandemonium, the high capital
Of Satan and his peers.   Their summons called
From every band and squarèd regiment
By place or choice the worthiest: they anon
With hundreds and with thousands trooping came   760
Attended.   All access was thronged; the gates
And porches wide, but chief the spacious hall
(Though like a covered field, where champions bold
Wont ride in armed, and at the Soldan's chair
Defied the best of Panim chivalry   765
To mortal combat, or career with lance),
Thick swarmed, both on the ground and in the air,
Brushed with the hiss of rustling wings.   As bees
In spring-time, when the sun with Taurus rides,
Pour forth their populous youth about the hive   770
In clusters; they among fresh dews and flowers
Fly to and fro, or on the smoothèd plank,
The suburb of their straw-built citadel,
New rubbed with balm, expatiate, and confer
Their state affairs: so thick the aery crowd   77
Swarmed and were straitened; till, the signal given,

The followers, at a signal, all contract: the leaders hold a council.

Behold a wonder!   They, but now who seemed
In bigness to surpass Earth's giant sons,
Now less than smallest dwarfs, in narrow room
Throng numberless—like that pygmean race   780
Beyond the Indian mount; or faery elves,
Whose midnight revels, by a forest side,
Or fountain, some belated peasant sees,
Or dreams he sees, while overhead the moon
Sits arbitress, and nearer to the Earth   785
Wheels her pale course: they, on their mirth and dance
Intent, with jocund music charm his ear;
At once with joy and fear his heart rebounds.
Thus incorporeal Spirits to smallest forms
Reduced their shapes immense, and were at large,   790
Though without number still, amidst the hall
Of that infernal court.   But far within,
And in their own dimensions like themselves,
The great Seraphic Lords and Cherubim
In close recess and secret conclave sat,   795
A thousand demigods on golden seats,
Frequent and full.   After short silence then,
And summons read, the great consult began.

NOTES.

[The letter (L.) *denotes that a word is used in its primary Latin sense; the letter* (G.) *that a further note, chiefly etymological, is given at p. 81.*]

1-5. Compare the opening lines of *Paradise Regained.*

1-3. For the prohibition, see vii. 323-333.

2. **mortal,** rendering liable to death.

> "The day thou eatst thereof, my sole command
> Transgressed, inevitably thou shalt die,
> From that day mortal."   vii. 329.

6. **Sing,** &c.   All preceding epic poets—Homer, Virgil, Dante, &c., use a similar form of invocation: in Milton's case it is a devout prayer for 'that impulse or voice of God by which the prophets were inspired'.

secret.   This term probably refers to the manner in which Moses received God's communications: see *Exodus* xix. 3, 12, 20; xxiv. 2 ("and Moses alone shall come near",) &c.

7. **Oreb** (Horeb), **or of Sinai.**   Milton refers either to *two* events—the appearance in the burning bush (*Exodus* iii.) and the giving of the Law—or, more probably, to the latter event alone, Sinai being a part of Horeb, a mountain group north of the Red Sea.

8. **that shepherd,** &c.   Moses, whose account of the creation is in *Genesis* i.   Cp. Psalm lxxvii. 20.

the chosen seed: the Jews considered themselves to be God's favoured people.

9. **the Heavens and Earth,** *i.e.* this Universe: see *Cosmology.*

10. **Sion hill,** where the Temple stood.

11. **Siloa's brook,** a stream flowing from the pool of Siloam into the Kidron, just beneath the city walls and very near the Temple ('the oracle', *1 Kings* vi.).

12. **fast by,** close to **oracle.**   (G.)

14. **middle,** either (1) mean, ordinary, or (2) more probably as in ll. 515-17, where the middle air denotes the air on the mountain tops.   Cp. 516 *n.*

15. **Aonia** (or Mt. Helicon) in Bœotia was the supposed abode of the nine Muses from whom the ancient poets sought inspiration. Cp. vii. 12-14, and ix. 1-47.

Milton means, therefore, either that he intends to surpass the ancient poets, Homer and Virgil, or that he intends to write on subjects higher than any they ever treated of.

15. **pursues**, treats of.   A Latinism.

16. **rhime** (properly *rime*), verse.   (G.)

18. Cp. *1 Corinthians* iii. 16.

19-22. Cp. *Genesis* i.; and for 'dove-like', *Matthew* iii. 16.

21. **Abyss**, lit. the bottomless depth (of the sea, &c.): here, *Chaos* (Gk.)

22. **pregnant**, filled with life.   Cp. vii. 234-42.

23. **low**, weak, feeble.

24. 'In a way befitting the subject of my poem.'
   highth, the correct form of the word: cp. depth, &c.

25. **assert**, defend in argument.

29. **grand parents**, first parents, ancestors.

32. **For one restraint**, &c., 'because of one restraint, being, in all else, lords', &c.   See 1-3 *n*.

33. **seduced**, led away from (allegiance, duty, &c.).   Cp. ii. 368, 'seduce them to our party'.

34. **infernal**, lit. belonging to the lower regions (or 'hell'): hence, wicked, fiendish.   But the word is also used without the notion of 'wicked': cp. "infernal court", 792.

35. For Satan's motives see i. 160-63, 651-54, ii. 348-51, 373, &c.

36. **what time**, when: cp. *Lycidas*, 28, "what time the gray-fly winds her sultry horn".

38. Note the extra syllable.

39. **peers**, equals.   Satan's 'peers' were his fellow-archangels. For the 'equality' see v. 659, &c.
   "He, of the first,
   If not the first Archangel, great in power,
   In favour and pre-eminence, yet fraught
   With envy against the Son of God", &c.;

and v. 812, where Abdiel addresses him—
   "In place so high above thy peers".

His crime, therefore, was his rivalry with God—his ambition to usurp the place of divine glory which belonged to God alone.

40. See v. 864; Satan, leading the revolt, declares—
   "Our puissance is our own; our own right hand
   Shall teach us highest deeds, by proof to try
   Who is our equal".

41. Ambitious. (G.)

43. impious, not pious, wanting in reverence to God.

45. flaming. Cp. *Luke* x. 18, "I beheld Satan as lightning fall from heaven"; and vi. 865-66.

ethereal sky, the Empyrean, or Heaven.

46. ruin, in its Latin sense, downfall.

combustion, confusion, uproar, tumult: lit. conflagration. See vi. 871.

> "Chaos roared
> And felt tenfold confusion in their fall
> Through his wild Anarchy". And cp. vi. 836-37 and 866.

48. adamantine, lit. made of adamant; that is, indestructible, unbreakable: cp. ii. 646, "adamantine rock...impenetrable,...unconsumed" by fire: and ii. 168, "we lay chained on the burning lake". The name 'adamant' was applied to steel and the diamond.

penal fire, fire used as a means of inflicting punishment. (L. *pœna,* pain.) Cp. 'penal laws', 'penalty', &c.

49. who, &c.: 'because he', 'since he', &c. A Latinism.

50. nine was a sort of sacred number with the ancients, as being a multiple of three. Cp. the use of the number seven in the Old Testament.

the space, &c. Why not simply 'nine days'?

51. crew, any company of men, as a ship's crew. Cp. Spenser, "A noble crew of lords and ladies".

53. confounded, stupefied, struck senseless.

55. pain: cp. vi. 327, "Then Satan first knew pain" (that is, in the war in heaven preceding the expulsion). For other references to the new consciousness of pain see 125, 147, 336, &c.

56. baleful, sorrowful. (*bale,* fr. A.S. *bale,* evil. Cp. Shak., *Coriolanus* i. 1. 66, "The one side must have bale".)

57. witnessed, bore witness to.

58. obdurate, immovable, unchangeable: lit. hardened. For the accent, cp. 'triúmphs' l. 123, 'sojoúrn" iii. 15, &c.

59. ken may be taken either as a verb or as a noun; if the latter, *angels* will be in the possessive case, either sing. or plural, as the mark of the possessive was in Milton's time often omitted. (M.E. *kennen,* to know.)

60. situation, region.

63. light: what is the case? Supply the verb.

darkness visible, &c. Cp. 181-83—

> "The seat of desolation, void of light,
> Save what the glimmering of these livid flames
> Casts pale and dreadful";

and *Il Penseroso*, 79, 80—

> "Where glowing embers through the room
> Teach light to counterfeit a gloom".

The language used in the text is contradictory only if taken literally—'the dungeon flamed', *i.e.* the flames were visible, but the dull 'glimmering' was only sufficient to reveal the prevailing horror and gloom. Mr. Beeching says, "The flame of a spirit-lamp in a dark room will suggest what is meant". Cp. also *Job* x. 22.

63. darkness visible, that is, gloom. Darkness is not itself visible any more than silence is audible. [What figure of speech is 'darkness visible', taken literally?]

66, 67. '(where) hope, that comes to all (mortals), never comes.' The thought is found in Euripides: and Dante (*Inferno* iii.) has the famous inscription over the gates of hell, "All hope abandon, ye who enter here".

68. still, ever, constantly.

urges, torments, harasses. A Latinism. Cp. ii. 88–89, "pain...must exercise us".

68, 69. Note the order—epithet, substantive, epithet. (Give other instances of this favourite idiom of Milton's.) Burning sulphur is fluid: hence 'deluge', flood.

71. those rebellious (angels) : cp. 521.

72. utter, outer, further from Heaven, hence belonging to Hell ; the intervening being the 'middle' darkness. Cp. iii. 16, "through utter and through middle darkness".

74. That is, three times the distance from the centre of this Universe (the Earth) to the outside sphere (the Primum Mobile), or else to its point of suspension from the Empyrean. For this use of 'centre', cp. 686–87. On the position of the Universe in space, see *Cosmology*, p. 21.

78. weltering, rolling about. In the Bible of 1549 we read, "He that weltereth a stone"; in the version of 1610, "He that rolleth a stone". (*Proverbs* xxvi. 27.)

80. Palestine, for Philistia, the coast district to the south-west of Palestine. So also in 465.

79-81. Beëlzebub, or Baalzebub, lit. 'lord of flies', was a god of the Philistines. His chief temple was at Ekron; his wishes were probably interpreted by the humming and motions of flies. For "next in crime" (79) see note on l. 88.

82. Satan (Hebrew) enemy: his former name was Lucifer ('light-bearer'). Cp. vii. 131.

84. beëst, indicative mood (=art). In A. S. there were two forms of the present indicative of the verb 'be'.

how fallen. Cp. *Isaiah* xiv. 12 ; and see p. 85.

86. transcendent, surpassing.

didst : note the syntax.

88. United thoughts, &c. See v. 676, &c.
Beëlzebub was Satan's first 'associate' in the rebellion. He seems to have been won over at once, and to have obeyed the prime mover implicitly. As his 'next subordinate' he visits the subject Powers, ' tells, as he was taught', that they are all to assemble, "tells the suggested cause, and casts between ambiguous words...and jealousies, to sound or taint integrity" (v. 696).

93. He, the Son of God.

with his thunder. Cp. vi. 835, "in his right hand, Grasping ten thousand thunders, which he sent Before him", &c. ; and iii. 392.

94. for, on account of.

84-94. Note (1) the abrupt change in 84 ('but O', &c.), 92 and 93;
(2) the syntax of *didst* in 86, the antecedent being 'him'='who' ='thou';
(3) object to 'hath joined', viz. 'whom' in 87 ;
(4) the classical form of expression in 91–2, "thou seest into what pit we are fallen, and from what highth" ;
(5) the exact force of the phrase 'so much' in 92 ;
(6) the repeated use of the pronoun, as if to avoid mentioning God by name, *e.g.* in 93. So cp. all the speeches in i. and ii.
(7) the want of continuity in sense and the absence of any regular principal clause in the passage.
These are the first words uttered after the expulsion from Heaven, and Milton evidently intends to indicate the speaker's excitement.

97. lustre, splendour, brightness; a shining appearance. (Low L. *lustrum,* a window.)

98. 'Lofty pride springing from the feeling that his merit had been despised.'

injured, despised. (L.) Cp. 500 *n.*

99, 100. Note 'contend' and its cognate 'contention'.

102. dislike, disapprove : not to 'dislike' in our sense of the word: the latter does not depend upon our 'daring', the former may.

104. dubious, for a time uncertain as to the result: the battle lasted three days. See Book vi.

105. shook his throne: what figure?

107. Study of, in its L. sense, a desire for, or, perhaps, pursuit of.

109. 'And in what else (*i.e.* besides these qualities) does not being overcome consist?' The line is, properly, parenthetical, or explanatory: and in some editions was printed in brackets. 'That glory', then, refers directly to 'submit or yield'.

Some editors, however, put a semicolon after 'overcome', so that the line means 'and whatever other qualities are invincible', or 'in whatever besides invincibility consists'.

112. suppliant, bent. (L.)

deify, exalt into an object of worship.

114. doubted his empire, felt insecure in regard to his supremacy. (Empire; L. *imperium*, rule, sway.)

116. by fate, &c. Satan regards the angels as equal to God in all but power (hence 'gods'), and equally free; not created by the Almighty, but, like Him, self-formed and immortal. For Satan's view of their origin, cp. v. 853, &c.

fate, necessity, the nature of things, regarded as unalterable and beyond the power of God. Cp. vii. 172—

"Necessity and Chance
Approach not me; and what I will is Fate".

117. this empyreal substance. The four elements, according to the ancients, were earth, air, fire, and water. Of these 'fire' was considered the noblest, and of it the angels, the heavens, &c., were supposed to be formed, whereas man was formed of 'earth'. Cp. 137-139. (Gk. *pur*, fire.)

120. more successful hope, hope that is likely to prove more fortunate, to lead to better success.

123. triumphs: either an iambic (trium'phs) or a spondee (tri'um'phs).

124. tyranny. In ancient Greece a tyrant was a man who usurped the supreme authority, and governed at will. He was not *necessarily* a bad ruler. It is probably in a neutral sense that *tyranny* is used here. To what contemporary event may Milton be alluding?

125. apostate, as adj., false, traitorous: lit. one who deserts (his religion, party, &c.).

126. vaunting, boasting: connected with *vain*.

racked, tortured: lit. 'put on the rack'.

127. compeer, an associate or companion of equal rank.

128. throned powers, *i.e.* powers of high rank: cp. 360*n*, and see p. 19.

129. Parse led. embattled, arranged in order of battle.

130. conduct, leadership.

132. 'And put it to the proof whether His supremacy was upheld, &c'. For *fate*, cp. 116.

133. For **chance,** cp. ii. 907, &c.—"Chaos umpire sits,...next him, high arbiter, Chance governs all": and ii. 960-65.

134. event, outcome, issue, result (of the 'proof'). (L.)

138. essences, beings.

139. remains: why singular?

141. glory: in what did this consist? See ll. 84-6, 97, 591-94, 610-12. Hence note the exact force and appropriateness of 'extinct'.

144. of force, either perforce, of necessity; or depending on 'almighty'.

146. have: what mood, and why?

148. suffice, satisfy.

149. mightier service—*i.e.* than we could render if our strength were diminished.

152. the gloomy deep, Chaos.

156. fiend, lit. hater, enemy. Cp. Satan, 82 *n.*

162. providence, foresight.

165. so as, 'to such a degree that'.

167. if I fail not, if I am not mistaken. Lat. *ni fallor.*

169, 170. The angry Victor, the Son; **his ministers**, the good angels. But according to Book vi. the Son alone drove out the rebels, and the good angels had taken part in the preceding war only. The difficulty is easily explained. Either Satan, as a rebel, did not know of the change, or he was unwilling to acknowledge the Son's superior might. Cp. vi. 801 and 880, and ii. 77-9 and 996-98.

172. laid, stilled, calmed. 'The storm of hail having blown over, the fiery waves become calm.'

176. his, masculine, as 'Thunder' is personified. (At this time (c. 1660) 'its' was just coming into use as the neuter of 'his'. In the Bible of 1610 'its' occurs only once (*Leviticus* xxv. 5), in Milton's poems only four or five times.)

177. vast, extensive, perhaps with the notion of waste, desolate.

178. slip, let slip (transitive). Cp. *Macbeth*, "I...slipt the hour", and such current phrases as 'slip a cable', &c.

179. satiate, satiated, satisfied; so 'uplift' or uplifted in 193.

yield, what mood, and why?

185. harbour, dwell, find a lodging-place. (A *harbour* was a lodging-place for the officers of an army—Low Latin, *heribergum*: Ger. *heer*, an army, and *bergen*, to shelter. Remains of old Roman villas on the great Roman roads were often used by travellers in later times as inns, and were called Cold Harbours; the name still survives in about fourteen places in England. A *harbinger* was a person who went on in advance to prepare a *harbour*.)

186. afflicted, in its Latin sense, flung or dashed down, crushed.

powers, forces, armies.

187. offend, harm. (L.)

197. fables, in the classical sense, stories of heathen heroes and deities.

198–200. (whether) Titanian or Earth-born. The *Titans* were the twelve sons of Uranus and Ge (*i.e.* Heaven and Earth); the *Earth-born*, offspring of the same parents, were the Giants. According to the legends the Giants made war on Jove, and were destroyed for their insolence. *Briareos* was one of the Titans, Typhon one of the Giants. The latter was supposed to dwell in a cave in Cilicia (in Asia Minor), which Milton denotes by Tarsus, its capital.

In 510, Milton speaks of "Titan, Heaven's first-born, with his enormous brood". There is no individual Titan known. But the legends do not agree with one another.

201. Leviathan, &c. The description fits the whale—except the 'scaly rind' (206): the name (Hebrew) is found in Job xli., and seems to be applied to the crocodile: but in other passages of Scripture, as in Ps. civ. 26, to any sea-monster.

203. ocean stream: in Homeric times the ocean was regarded as a stream encircling the (flat) earth, and connected with 'the Sea' (the Mediterranean) in the East and in the West. Scan the line.

203–207. Olaus Magnus, a Swede (in his *History of the Northern Nations*, 1658), and other writers of Milton's time, tell of the whale's being taken for an island by sailors, who anchor to his back, drive stakes into him, &c. Milton speaks of him as 'like a promontory' (vii. 414); *four acres* in extent, says another writer!

204. pilot, captain.

night-foundered, lost in the darkness, stopped by the night coming on. (Strictly, *founder* means to *sink*.)

skiff, ship. (Now the word denotes a small boat.)

207. under the lee, on the side (of the whale) protected from the wind. What is the other side called? (M.E. *lee*, also *lew*, shelter.)

208. Invests, enshrouds, wraps (like a garment). (L. *vestis*, a garment.)

wished. Note similar omissions of prepositions in 282 ('fallen'), 660 ('despaired'), 662 ('resolved'), &c.

196–210. What figure of speech is employed here? What feature of the Fiend is it intended to emphasise?

210. Cp. *2 Peter* ii. 4, and *Jude* 6.

211. Had, would have.

214. reiterated, repeated again and again. (L. *re*, and *iterum*, again.)

215. damnation, punishment: see 219 and 220.

219. sĕduced, led away from duty and virtue.

226. incumbent, lying, leaning, or resting his weight on.

230-37. What is the passage meant to describe, and by what figure? Comparing it with 196-210, is it more or less effective, and why?

230. (What was the hue?)

230, 231. Note the peculiar assumption in this passage as to the cause of earthquakes.

232. Pelorus, now Cape Faro, N.E. of Sicily. It is near Etna. Probably 'from' governs 'shattered side'.

234. fuelled, full of fuel.

234-37. thence, &c. 'The contents of the mountain catching fire from this wind are changed into vapour by a heat like that of molten metals, and, in their turn, increase the force of the wind'. (Properly, *subliming* is a chemical operation in which volatile solids are separated from impurities, by heating, just as liquids are purified by distillation.) (L. *sublimis*, aloft, in the air.) **involved,** enveloped. (L.)

238. unblest feet: note the figure of speech and the exact force of *unblest*.

239. glorying, boasting. (L.)

Stygian, hateful, horrible. Cp. 195. The Styx ('hateful'), of the classical mythology, was the chief river in the lower world.

241. supernal, above. (L. *super, supernus.*)

242. clime, probably climate, temperature, as if 'region' referred to the *position,* '*clime*' to the *kind* of country.

244. Note the peculiar use of **change**—like L. *muto.*

246. sovran, O.F. *soverain,* Ital. *sovrano,* L. *superanus.* A more correct form than *sovereign*—confused with *reign.*

246, 247. dispose and bid What shall be right, 'make his own will the standard of right and wrong'—*justum est id quod jussum est.*

247-49. 'Furthest from him is best for us; for though we are his equals in reason, we are inferior to him in strength.' Cp. 92-4, and 144-45.

251. Infernal (from L. *infra, infernus*), 'very low', without the notion of 'wicked'. Cp. 251, 657, 792.

253. Cp. Horace, "Caelum non animum mutant qui trans mare currunt".

253-56. Cp. iv. 20-23, and iv. 75, "which way I fly is Hell, my-self am Hell". Note the rare form 'its', found only three or four times in Milton. Cp. 176 *n.*

257. 'What I should be, in all respects except that I am inferior to Him in power.'

259-61. 'This place at any rate is free from his envy.' Note the emphatic position of 'here' and 'hence'.

261. secure, in its then usual sense, free from anxiety. (L. *se*, apart from, and *cura*, care.) See 638 *n.*

266. astonished, stunned, 'astounded' (281), 'confounded' (53), 'entranced' (301). Lit., struck senseless.

oblivious, causing forgetfulness. Cp. *Macbeth*, "oblivious antidote"; and 'forgetful lake', ii. 74. Milton is thinking of the river Lethe, of the classical mythology, which caused all who drank of it to forget the past.

268. mansion, place of abode. (L. *mansum*, to dwell.)

273. foiled, defeated. (M.E. *foylen*, O.F. *fouler*, to trample under foot.) Quite distinct from *foil*, anything used to set off a gem. (L. *folium*, a leaf.)

274. pledge, surety.

274, 275. liveliest pledge Of hope, giving life to hope.

276, 277. perilous edge of battle, either the front line of battle (L. *acies*), or at the critical moment. For the former sense, cp. vi. 108 :—

> "Before the cloudy van
> On the rough edge of battle ere it joined,
> Satan with vast and haughty strides advanced".

281. astounded, same as astonished. See 266.

amazed, in a stronger sense than that in which it is now used: bewildered, dazed. (From *maze*.)

282. fallen: cp. 208 *n.*

pernicious, destructive, ruinous. (L. *perniciosus*.)

285. Ethereal temper, (a thing) wrought in Heaven, of heavenly workmanship. Cp. iv. 812 :—

> "No falsehood can endure
> Touch of celestial temper" (*i.e.* Ithuriel's spear), &c.

(*Temper*, to bring to the proper degree of hardness, to mix metals in due proportion. L. *temperare*, to regulate.)

288. artist, a professor of an art; it also denoted a skilled worker, our 'artisan'. The 'Tuscan artist' is Galileo (1564-1642), a teacher of mathematics and astronomy at Pisa. His improvements in the telescope—for he did not invent it—enabled him to make discoveries which convinced him of the truth of the Copernican theory of astronomy. (See p. 22.) He was tried twice by the Inquisition for holding 'erroneous' opinions, and silenced. He was living near Florence, 'a prisoner to the Inquisition, for thinking in astronomy otherwise than the licensers thought', when Milton visited him in 1638–39. He had become blind in 1636. In v. 262, he is mentioned by name.

289, 290. Fesolè, now Fiesolè, is a hill near Florence. **Valdarno**, i.e. Val d'Arno, the valley in which Florence is situated.

291. spotty, refers to the dark patches in the moon; they are the shadows cast by the mountains. It was Galileo that discovered the unevenness of the moon's surface. In v. 420 Milton attributes the 'spots' to the presence of vapour. It is now generally agreed that there are no *rivers* (nor vapour) in the moon.

292. to equal which, compared with which.

294. ammiral, the chief ship of a fleet, so called from its carrying the superior officer. (Arabic, *amir*, ruler, cp. *ameer*, and *al*, the.)

296. marle, ground; properly a soft, rich soil. Cp. 562.

297. Heaven's azure, the crystal floor of Heaven.

299. Nathless, none the less; now displaced by *nevertheless*. The word is common in Chaucer.

300. inflamed, in its literal sense, burning, in flames.

301. entranced. (G.) What other terms are used to describe their conditions?

303. Vallombrosa ('shady valley'), a beautiful and thickly wooded valley and hilly slope about 18 miles from Florence. It is said that Milton spent several days at a monastery that stood here.

Etruria, Tuscany.

304. imbower, form bowers.

sedge, in Hebrew the Red Sea is called 'the sedgy sea', on account of the large quantity of sea-weed found in it.

305. Orion (Orīon), a constellation so named from a companion of Artemis or Diana, the goddess of hunting. The time of year at which this constellation sets—November or early December—was generally associated by the poets with bad weather.

"Quam multi Libyco volvuntur marmore fluctus
Saevus ubi Orion hibernis conditur undis."
Virgil, *Aeneid*, vii. 218–19.

(Give other instances of poetical traditions in this Book.)

armed, some of the stars of Orion appear to be arranged in the form of a sword and belt.

307. Busiris, here identified with the Pharaoh of *Exodus*.

Memphian, Egyptian, from the ancient capital Memphis, on the west bank of the Nile.

chivalry, army— horse and foot, though in this case mainly horse. (*Exodus*, xiv. 28.) Doublet 'cavalry'. See 575 *n*. on *infantry* and *cavalry*.

308. perfidious. Pharaoh had given the Israelites permission to leave Egypt.

309. sojourners, temporary dwellers in a place. (O.F. *sojourner*, fr. L. *diurnus*, fr. *dies*, a day.)

Goshen, a district east of the delta of the Nile.

who beheld, &c. See *Exodus* xxiv. 30.

311. so...abject and lost—as what? Analyse the similes in lines 302-13. With 309-12 cp. 323-25.

abject, cast down.

318-22. Or...or, whether...or.

virtue, valour, bravery: lit. manliness. (L. *vir*.) Scan l. 318: which word is made emphatic?

320, 321. See v. 640, &c., for the evening 'repast' and slumbers of the angels.

322. sworn To adore the Conqueror. In both questions Satan is taunting them: 'They had previously risked all rather than do this—were they going to give in now?'

324. Cherub and Seraph, the two kinds of angels, 'angels of love and angels of light': see p. 19. Of course the reference here is to Satan's followers—under their former names. Cp. 157, 'Fallen Cherub'.

325. ensigns, standards, distinguishing marks or signs. (L. *insignia*.)

till. The construction is abrupt: supply 'and will continue to watch us' before *till*.

326. His pursuers: what kind of genitive, objective or subjective?

337. obey, in M.E. took a dative case. (Cp. Fr. *obéir à*.)

338, &c. Alluding to Moses and the plagues. See *Exodus* x. 12, &c.

341. warping. (1) This is usually regarded as a peculiar use of the nautical term 'warp', that is, to haul a ship forward, by means of a cable fixed some distance ahead. But this would not produce the zigzag course required by the usual explanation—'an undulatory forward motion' of a large mass. (2) Is not the word more probably used in the sense of 'floating about' at the mercy of the wind,

like the Ark in the Flood? Compare the following passage from
The Deluge, a poem of the 13th century :—

(The Ark) " luged about
Where the wind and the weder *warpen* hit wolde ".

345. cope, roof, vault. Cp. iv. 992, "Starry cope of heaven".
(Cp. *cap* and *cape*.)

347. the uplifted...waving. What is the construction?

348. sultan (or *soldan*, 764), victor, prince: in 378 'emperor'.

350. brimstone, *i.e.* 'burning stone': why?

351-55. The Goths, from the province of Dacia, north of the
Danube (*Danaw*), pressed forward by the Huns, settled in ' the
Empire' in 376; soon afterwards they defeated the Romans in
battle. Forty years later the west Goths sacked Rome, and some
passed into Gaul and Spain. German tribes too were at this time
crossing the Rhine (*Rhene*), and pressing on into Gaul and Spain.
Hordes of Huns now attacked Romans, Goths, and Germans alike,
but were defeated in 451 at Châlons—one of the world's critical
battles. Some Germans called Vandals, who had at first settled in
Spain, crossed into Africa (*Libya*) in 429, and founded a kingdom,
with Carthage as capital. Even in Italy some east Goths settled.
From these various settlements the *Romance* nations sprung.

356. squadron, lit. 'that which is squared'. (It. *squadrone*, L.
esquadratum.) Cp. 758, 'squared regiments and bands'.

360. erst, superl. of *ere*; once, at first.

For **thrones,** cp. 128 and 737 *n.*

362. rased, for 'erased'. What is the difference? (L. *rasum*,
scrape.)

363. Books of Life. *Revelation* iii. 5.

370. Glory—what is the case?

372. religions, decorations. So, in Shakespeare's *Julius Cæsar*,
the statues of Cæsar are "decked with ceremonies".

358-375. Milton assumes the belief of the early Christian Church
that the Pagan gods were fallen angels in disguise. In *Par. Reg.*
(*e.g.* II. 121–6) he identifies the fallen angels with the ' demons' of
the four elements.

380. promiscuous, mixed, confused.

382. Cp. *1 Peter* v. 8, "Your adversary the devil...walketh
about, seeking whom he may devour."

383. seat of God, the Temple at Jerusalem.

385, 386. durst abide, stood their ground in spite of. Cp. 470.

thundering out of Sion, referring perhaps to what was
thundered (the ten commandments, one of which forbad idolatry).

387. Cherubim, two figures in the sanctuary of the Temple. *1 Kings* vi. 23.

388. shrines, altars. See *2 Kings* xxi. 4, "And he (*i.e.* King Manasseh) built altars in the house of the Lord." (G.)

389. abominations: referring to the idolatrous character of the shrines.

390. profaned, defiled, made unholy, desecrated. (L. *profanus*, unholy; lit. before (or outside of) a temple, *fanum*.)

392-521. See the Table of Heathen Deities, p. 77.

394. Timbrel, a kind of tambourine.

403. that opprobrious hill, that hill of scandal (416), the offensive mountain (443), all refer to the Mt. of Olives, near Jerusalem. opprobrious. (G.)

404, 405. Hinnom was a deep narrow ravine bounding Jerusalem on the south-west. To put an end to the idol worship carried on there —with its human sacrifices—Josiah rendered it 'ceremonially unclean' by spreading human bones, &c., in it. Henceforward the refuse of the city was deposited there. By reason of its evil associations the later Jews used its name *Ge Hinnom* or *Gehenna*, to denote the place of torment. *Tophet* was the south-eastern part of the valley. Here, facing the city on the 'hill of scandal', Solomon erected his high places to Moloch. (Smith's *Bible Dict.*)

406. obscene, foul, repulsive.

414, 415. wanton rites = lustful orgies. The worship of some of the heathen deities was attended with all kinds of wild excesses, drunkenness, &c. (Cp. the account of the offering to Baal in *1 Kings* xviii. 28.) wanton, wild, unrestrained. (G.). orgies, originally ceremonies observed in the worship of Bacchus (god of wine), distinguished by furious revelry. (Gk. *orgé*, fury.) (G.)

417. homicide. (G.)

419. bordering flood, because forming the south or south-west boundary of Canaan. *Genesis* xv. 18.

423. feminine for 'female'.

424. soft, pliable, able to take any shape.

424, 425. so soft And uncompounded, &c. Milton regards the Angels as 'pure intelligential substances', pure spirit—that is, as beings possessing mental powers of various kinds, but unconnected with a material body.
They require nutriment (Raphael explains to Adam), just as we rational beings do, digesting, assimilating, and turning the material substance into immaterial. See v. 407-8, 438, 497; and vi. 350—

> " All heart they live, all head, all eye, all ear,
> All intellect, all sense; and as they please
> They limb themselves, and colour, shape, or size
> Assume as likes them best, condense or rare".

424, 425. essence pure, then, is the immaterial angelic substance,—conceived as of the same character throughout (homogeneous), like perfectly pure water, or pure oxygen; *uncompounded* denotes the absence of composite organs or groups—like the heart, &c., in man—and hence its freedom to take any particular form.

426. manacled, lit. handcuffed: not limited in their movements, size, or shape by joints and limbs. (*Manacle*, a handcuff, from L.)

427. founded, built upon as a foundation. What does 'brittle' qualify? What is the figure?

in what shape: note instances.

429. obscure, dark, shadowy.

430. aery, in or through the air.

435. bestial, refers either to the grossness of their worship, or to 476–89 below. In Egypt the sacred bulls "maintained...in the great temples of their respective cities were perpetually adored and prayed to by thousands during their lives, and at their deaths were entombed with the utmost care in huge sarcophagi, while all Egypt went into mourning for them" (Rawlinson).

436. Parse bowed and sunk.

438. Astoreth or Ashtoreth (singular form of Ashtaroth), representing the moon, which might be considered the fainter reflection or wife of the sun, and was, as the moon, addressed as 'queen of heaven'. *Jeremiah* vii. 18. (Sayce).

439. crescent horns, the horns of the crescent moon.

441. paid their vows and songs: What figure of speech is this?

444. uxorious, referring to his having many wives.

455. See *Ezekiel* viii. 14, "Then he brought me to the door of the gate of the Lord's house,...and behold, there sat women weeping for Tammuz".

456. dark, wicked, horrible.

457. alienated, estranged. (L. *alienus*, strange, foreign.)

458. in earnest, *i.e.* as compared with the mourning of the Jewish women for Tammuz.

460. grunsel, *i.e.* groundsill or threshold.

479. abused, deceived and enticed.

480. Fanatic, superstitious, raving. See 435 *n*. (L. *fanaticus*, fr. *fanum*, a temple.)

485. Jeroboam, King of Israel, who rebelled against Rehoboam, set up two golden calves.

486. grazed, fed on grass.

(M 46)　　　　　　　　　　　　　　E

487-89. As the Israelites were on the point of leaving Egypt, a plague fell equally on the first-born of the Egyptians and on the animals which they worshipped.

bleating: one of their gods was represented as a ram, another as a goat, but the chief (Apis) as a bull. See *Exodus* xii. 29.

491. gross, depraved.

495. *I Samuel* ii. 12 and 22.

497-502. In these lines Milton is thought to be referring to the dissolute state of London and of the court after the Restoration. (See Macaulay, *History*, i. 360.)

500. injury, wrong, wrong-doing—not 'damage'. (L. *injuria*; opposed to *jus*, what is right or lawful.)

502. flown, flushed.

503. *Genesis* xix.

504. *Judges* xix. 25.

hospitable door: what is the figure?

508. Javan's issue, *i.e.* the Greeks, regarded as descended from *Javan* or *Ion*, son of Japhet. (*Genesis* x. 2, *Isaiah* lxvi. 19.)

509. confessed, worshipped.

510. Titan, see 198 *n.*

514, 515. Ida, a mountain in Crete, and the birthplace of Zeus.

515, 516. Olympus, the fabled abode of the Greek gods, is a mountain in Thessaly; its highest point is covered with snow most of the year.

middle air. Mr. Verity suggests that in the middle ages the atmosphere was regarded as made up of three regions; and that this 'middle air' is the cold region of clouds and heavy vapours about the mountain tops.

517, 518. Delphi, at the foot of the steep southern slope of Mount Parnassus; **Dodōna**, in Epirus. These were the seats of the two most famous oracles of ancient Greece—of Apollo and Zeus respectively.

520, 521. Vergil and Ovid both speak of Saturn as fleeing alone (over the Hadriatic Sea) before his son Zeus, to Italy, called by the Greeks the Hesperian (or western) fields.

521. the Celtic (fields), the western or Celtic parts of the Continent, especially France.

(to) **the utmost isles**, probably Britain, &c.

523. damp, depressed. Cp. 'to damp a fire', 'to damp one's spirits'. What is the figure?

524. Obscure, faintly, indistinctly.

525, 526. not lost in loss itself, *i.e.* in what seemed likely to prove absolute destruction. What is the figure?

527. Like doubtful hue: explain 'doubtful'.

528. recollecting, re-collecting, recovering.

529. gently, either without harshness, or gallantly, nobly.

530. fainting: in first edition 'fainted'.

532. clarions, clear-sounding horns. (L. *clarus.*) (Skeat.)

534. Azazel, probably the name of some evil spirit. The word means 'the solitary one', or 'the scape-goat'. See *Leviticus* xvi. 8: "And Aaron shall cast lots upon the two goats; one lot for the Lord, and the other lot for the scape-goat" ('Azazel', R.V.).

536. advanced, raised, uplifted. **Ensign.** (G.)

537. meteor. (G.)

538. golden lustre, lustrous gold.

emblazed, richly adorned, like a shield. To *blazon* is to portray armorial bearings on a shield. (M. E. *blason*, a shield.) Cp. v. 588: "Ensigns high advanced...in their glittering tissue, bear emblazed holy memorials." The word is an heraldic term.

539. arms, probably the ensign itself; **trophies,** gems and gold, regarded as symbols of victory.

540. martial, warlike. (L. *Mars, Martis*, the god of war.)

541. universal, in its Latin sense, whole, entire.

542. concave, hollow roof, or vault.

543. reign, kingdom, realm. Cp. "Pluto's grisly reign", Spenser; and later, Gray's Elegy, "molest her ancient solitary reign".

Chaos, &c., see ii. 890–967, where Night is spoken of as 'eldest of things', and 'eldest Night and Chaos' as ancestors of Nature, because they preside over that out of which 'things' are formed.

546. orient (from L. *oriens, orientis*, the east, the rising sun), constantly used as an epithet of gems. It is frequently used by Milton in the sense of 'bright', 'clear', 'shining'

547. forest huge: what figures?

helms, helmets.

548. serried (as if) joined or locked together. (F. from L. *serere*, to join.) This appearance might be caused by the regularity of the lines and the uniform stature of the troops.

550. phalanx. "A body of troops in close array with a long spear as their principal weapon. It was among the Dorians, and especially among the Spartans that this arrangement was most rigidly adhered to." (Smith's *Dict. of Antiquities.*)

to the Dorian mood, *i.e.* to music of a grave, severe character, supposed to inspire courage and endurance, as distinguished from the Lydian or soothing, tender music (cp. *L'Allegro*, 139), and trumpet music (540-41). mood. (G.)

551. flutes and soft recorders. The modern flute is of recent German origin: the flute of Milton's day—the English flute—was called a recorder. As he is speaking of Greek music, the expression probably refers in general terms to the so-called flutes of the Greeks, which included reed instruments. They were of various sizes, and the different parts of the harmony—bass, tenor, &c.—could be played on them.

551, 552. 'Such as infused the highest courage and endurance into heroes', &c.

temper, disposition, temperament, frame of mind. Cp. 285 *n.*, and ii. 276.

554. breathed, infused, inspired, instilled.

556. mitigate, make soft, mild, less severe. (L. *mitis.*)

swage (assuage), soothe, soften: lit. to make sweet. (L. *suavis.*)

557. touches, strains. Cp. Shakespeare, *Merchant of Venice*, v. 57—
"Here let the sounds of music
Creep in our ears; soft stillness and the night
Become the touches of sweet harmony".

561. Cp. vi. 61.

charmed, in its old sense, denoting the effect of some mysterious power or influence—as here, fascinated by means of music. (L. *carmen*, a song.)

563. horrid, in its Latin sense, bristling (with spears). Cp. 'Horrid hair', ii. 710.

front, line.

568. traverse, across, athwart.

569. due, correct, proper, suitable. One of Milton's favourite words.

570. stature: why singular? Cp. 778.

573. since created man, since the creation of man. A Latin idiom. Cp. 797-98, "After.. summons read".

574. embodied force, an army massed.

named, compared.

575. merit (more regard), 'be of more account'.

infantry. In the middle ages, the cavalry were considered as forming the main body of the army; and the two terms 'cavalry' and 'army' were convertible. Cp. chivalry, 307. The foot-men or infantry were deemed little better than rabble (Trench); and probably the word is used in this contemptuous sense here. (Span. and It. *infanta*, a child, a servant, a foot-soldier.)

The reference here is to the Pygmies (cp. 780) a fabulous race whose stature was a '*pugmé*' (about 13½ in.). They are said by Homer to have been attacked by cranes every spring, and according to the legends they fought on the backs of rams and partridges.

576-87. Milton refers to three groups of oes: Greek, British, and Mediæval.

576-79. The Greek gods and heroes.

Phlegra, the westernmost of the three small peninsulas lying to the east of the Gulf of Salonica; the scene of the war between the gods and the giants. See 198.

Thebes and Ilium. 'The heroic race that fought at Thebes and Ilium' symbolizes the great heroes of Greek literature and legendary history.

The story of the exploits of The Seven (Greeks) against Thebes is told by Aeschylus, the story of the Trojan war by Homer.

Troy in N.-W. Asia Minor.

Thebes in Bœotia.

auxiliar gods refers to the part taken by the deities in the siege of Troy. (L. *auxilium*, help.)

579-581. Legendary British heroes.

Uther's (or Uther Pendragon's) son, *i.e.* King Arthur, assisted by knights of Britain and of Brittany. For some time (about 1638-39) Milton had thought of taking the Arthurian legends as the subject of his great poem.

582-87. Mediæval (historical) heroes.

Jousted, tilted; joust, literally, is the *jostling* together of two knights on horseback at a tournament. (Low L. *juxtare*, to meet.)

baptized, Christians. infidel, one who does *not* accept the Christian *faith*—hence, Moors, Mahomedans, &c.

583, 584. The names in these lines are said by some critics to have been taken by Milton at random; but Mr. Verity holds that each one was carefully selected for its associations with the mediæval romances of chivalry, by which Milton in his youth had been greatly attracted.

The names are in any case symbolical, like Thebes and Ilium

above; at the same time some of them may be connected with particular events.

Aspramont, a castle near Nice. ⎫ All familiar names in the old
Damasco.   ⎬ romances, and specially associ-
Trebisond, a town of great note ⎪ ated with tournaments and
and splendour in the middle ages. ⎭ jousts.

Damasco was also the scene of several battles in the Crusades.

Montalban, a castle in Languedoc, of note in the wars of Charlemagne.

Marocco, Biserta, associated with the wars between the Christians (Spaniards) and the Moors. From Biserta (the ancient Utica, near Carthage) a Moorish army started to attack the Christians under Charlemagne in Spain; the defeat, however, was inflicted not by the Moors but by the Gascons at Roncesvalles, 'by Fontarabbia', near Biarritz. (Charlemagne was not killed in the battle in 778: he lived till 814.)

586. all his peerage, i.e. the brave Roland, the wise Oliver, and all the rest of the twelve peers or paladins of France—except perhaps one.

587. 'Thus far these surpassed mortals: yet they obeyed', &c. Explain 'thus far'.

588. observed, obeyed. Cp. 'to observe a command'.

592, 593. 'Nor did it appear less (noble and commanding) than that of an archangel who was now fallen and his excessive brightness dimmed.'

595. horizontal, level, lying towards the horizon.

597–99. disastrous, unfavourable, of bad omen. (G.) Cp. *Julius Cæsar*, ii. 2. 30:—

" When beggars die, there are no comets seen,
The heavens themselves blaze forth the death of princes ".

598. Why 'half the nations'?

594–600. What point is this simile meant to illustrate?

600. Archangel. (G.)

601. Scars of thunder, i.e. made by the lightning.

intrenched, marked, furrowed, cut into.

603. considerate, meditating (revenge), planning, scheming.

604. 'His eye was cruel but showed', &c.

605. Remorse, self-reproach: lit. 'a biting again'. (L. *re-mordeo*.)

Passion, suffering, sorrow: not as now, *strong* feeling only.

606. Were they *fellows* or *followers*? See 88 *n*. and v. 805, &c.

609. amerced, deprived (by way of fine or punishment). (O.F. *amercier*, to fine; from L. *mercedem*.)

611. 'Yet he beheld how, nevertheless, they stood faithful', &c.

613. scathed, injured, damaged.

614. singed: does lightning merely singe the tops of trees?

615. blasted, withered, blighted, by the lightning. The expression 'blasted heath' occurs in *Macbeth* i. 3. 77. It is the meeting-place of Macbeth and the witches in the *thunder-storm*.

618. peers, the chiefs previously mentioned in 391–521.

619. assayed, tried.

thrice, see 50 *n*.

in spite of scorn, though scorning to weep.

622–26. Cp. the beginning of his first speech, ll. 84–87. Note how much is implied in the phrase, 'but with the Almighty'.

622. myriads. (G.)

624. event, outcome, result.

627. presaging, half-expecting, surmising: lit. foreseeing.

628. 'knowledge (of the) past', &c.

628, 629. could have feared How, 'could have had any fear that such', &c., or 'could have known any reasons for fearing', &c.

632. exile, note the accent. **puissant**, mighty. **legion.** (G.)

Hath emptied: what figure? Cp. ii. 692. (Satan "drew after him the third part of Heaven's sons".)

633. reascend, *re*, back (not 'again').

634. self-raised. Cp. ii. 75–7.

636. counsels different (from those of the rest), 'divided counsels'.

dangers shunned, the shunning of dangers.

637. lost, destroyed.

638. secure, free from care or misgiving (with regard to his supremacy). Cp. Ben Jonson: "Men may securely sin, but safely never"; and l. 261: "Here we may reign secure".

643, 645. our better part: 'henceforth our safest course is', &c.

646. close, secret. Cp. 795.

647. no less, 'that he may learn from us as we have learnt from him, that he who overcomes', &c.

650, 651. so rife...fame, so general a rumour.

650–56. Cp. ii. 378–80. Note the importance of this suggestion and its results in Book ii.

656. eruption, sortie, expedition: lit. 'outbreak'.

657. infernal: see 241 *n.*

660–62. despaired, resolved: cp. 208 and note.

662. understood—amongst whom?

663. confirm, support, second, ratify.

668. This was the custom of Roman soldiers when applauding a general's speech. Note the expressiveness of this line through the repetition of the notion of sound in the words *clashed, sounding,* and *din.* Cp. 768.

670. grisly, horrible, hideous. Cp. ii. 704.

671. the rest entire, 'the rest being intact': or else, 'all the rest'.

672–4. scurf, flakes, flaky matter.

the work of sulphur. According to the alchemists, sulphur (understood as a vague 'principle of fixation', not the substance we call sulphur) was the chief agent in the formation of metals by its action on 'earth', on the 'seeds of metals', &c. The phrase work of sulphur refers to the metal either in the earth (as metallic ore) or cropping out (as a sulphide) in flakes on the surface (glossy scurf).

675. brigad. Cp. brigadier. (It. *brigata,* a troop.)

676. pioners. Pioneers clear the way for an army by making roads, &c. (From O.F. *peonier,* a foot-soldier; from Low L. *pedonem*: whence also 'pawn' in chess.)

677. camp, army. Cp. xi. 217, 'a camp of fire', *i.e.* 'chariots and horses of fire'.

678. cast, throw up.

Mammon (Syriac), riches, here used as a proper noun (like Belial, 490).

679. erected, high-minded, upright, noble.

682. *Revelation* xxi. 21.

683. else goes with aught.

684. vision beatific, a phrase used by early Christian writers to denote the 'sight of God', for which they hoped, and which was to give them perfect happiness. Cp. *Matthew* v. 8.

688. For treasures better hid, *i.e.* for gold, better left undisturbed.

690. admire, wonder. Cp. ii. 677–78. (L. *admirari.*)

692. precious, probably used contemptuously; if not, what is the figure in 'precious bane'? bane, harm.

694. Babel, probably Babylon, noted for its vast walls, its hanging gardens, and the Temple of Belus (720).

Memphian, Egyptian, as in 307, from *Memphis*, the ancient capital. Egypt was famous for its pyramids and for its temples of Serapis (720). In l. 718 the new city of Memphis is mentioned under the name *Alcairo*, the modern Cairo. Probably in the latter passage there is a repetition of line 694 under different names. Note that in the second passage Milton uses the more modern names, perhaps to suggest different aspects of the cities. But possibly *Babel* denotes the tower of Babel, and Memphian may be used in a much wider sense than Alcairo.

697. reprobate, base, depraved, lit. condemned. (L. *reprobare.*)

698, 699. Herodotus tells us that there were 366,000 men employed for twenty years in the building of the Great Pyramid.

702. Sluiced. A sluice is a sliding gate for regulating the flow of a liquid. (L. *exclusa*, shut-out.)

703. founded, melted. (L. *fundere*, to pour.) The process of purifying is now called smelting; whereas *founding* (705-7) denotes a later and final melting and moulding of the metal.

massy, heavy.

704. scummed, skimmed.

bullion refers to the unpurified metal ore. (L. *bullio*, a mass of metal; from *bullire*, to boil.)

dross, the impurities in the ore which float on the surface of the molten metal, forming a scum; so that *bullion-dross* is the scum that comes from the bullion.

706. various, elaborate, intricate; *e.g.* the frieze and the roof (706-7) would require such mouldings.

708, 709. All the pipes in an organ are supplied with wind from a wind-chest, of which the *sound-board* forms the upper part; the connecting channels, and the intricate mechanism by which they are controlled, are all hidden away in the depths of the instrument, and yet every single part answers to the easy touch of the player with a sureness and a promptness that make the organ truly magical, and lend far more force to this simile than might appear at first sight. Milton was very fond of the organ, and had one in his house.

710. Anon, presently.

711. Exhalation, a vapour or mist, suggestive of silence and ease. (L., lit. what is breathed out.) Cp. Tennyson—

"Like that strange song I heard Apollo sing,
While Ilion like a mist rose into towers".

712. dulcet symphonies, sweet accompanying chords or strains (on instruments).

713-17. like a temple. In Greece and in Asia Minor there were many temples, mostly Doric,' and their rows of pillars formed a conspicuous feature.

713. pilasters, square pillars partly sunk in a wall.

714. Doric pillars, round pillars of a massive, simple style, with plain capital. Cp. note on 'Dorian mood', 550. (The other two orders of pillars are Ionic—fluted, with voluted capitals; and Corinthian—lighter columns, with highly ornamented capitals.)

715. Architrave. The beam or stone-work which rests immediately on the top of a row of pillars; above it is an ornament called the *frieze*, and above that a projecting part called the *cornice*. Architrave means chief beam. (Gk. *arche*, and L. *trabs*.)

716. bossy, standing out prominently. (F. *bosse*, a knob.)

717. fretted, ornamented—properly with interlaced bars, like gratings. (O.F. *frete*. It. *ferata*, an iron-grating.)

717-20. See 694 *n.*

724, 725. 'Reveal, within, her wide and ample spaces', &c.

727. pendent, hung. (L. *pendeo*.) **magic.** (G.)

728. A cresset was a lamp consisting of a small, open, iron cage or vessel, in which was placed rope or tow steeped in pitch, &c. It was usually carried hanging from the top of a pole. (Fr. *creuset*, a pot; whence 'cruse' and 'cruet'.)

729. naphtha, a liquid distilled from petroleum; used for the lamps.

  asphaltus, pitch; used for the cressets.

730. Explain **hasty.**

737. In the middle ages it was supposed that the angels were of two kinds, Cherubim and Seraphim, or angels of light and angels of love, divided into three groups or **Hierarchies**, each consisting of three Orders. (Gk. *hierarches*, a ruler in sacred matters, a chief priest: cp. monarch.)

739. Ausonian land, Italy: from Ausonia, an ancient name for central Italy.

740. Mulciber, the softener, the metal-founder. (L. *mulcere*, to soften.) Another name for Vulcan, the Roman god of fire. In Greece he was called Hephæstus. He was smith and armourer to the gods of Olympus, and was represented as lame.

741. Why **fabled?** See 747, &c.

745. zenith, the highest point in the heavens over one's head. See also p. 20. What is the opposite point called?

746. Hence this island was sacred to Hephæstus, and here he had his forge!

747. rout, crowd, rabble (distinct from rout = defeat; from L. *rupta*).

750. engines, contrivances, ingenuity. (L. *ingenium*, skill, ingenuity.) Cp. Ben Jonson: "Sejanus worketh with all his ingine".

753. sovran. See 246 *n.*

aweful, awe-inspiring.

756. Pandemonium, the palace (or temple) 'of all the demons'. Cp. Pantheon, a Roman temple to all the gods.

758. squared regiment. Cp. 'perfect phalanx' (550), and 'squadron' (356).

761. access, note the meaning and accent.

764. wont, were accustomed. Past tense of A. S. *wunian*, to be accustomed.

765. Panim, belonging to a Pagan or heathen country.

766. career, the galloping of the combatants towards one another along the course. Note the two kinds of combat referred to; in the second the points of the lances were blunted. (F. *carrière*, a road, a horse race.)

768. What is there remarkable about this line? What does it suggest?

the hiss of wings, hissing wings. What is the figure?

769. In April the Sun traverses that part of the sky in which the constellation Taurus is situated.

771. fresh dews and flowers, *i.e.* fresh dewy flowers. So in v. 212: "Among sweet dews and flowers". What is the figure?

773. citadel, a little city—not a fort here. (Dim. of Italian *cittade*, or *città*, a city.)

774. balm, balsam; used by Milton of any fragrant resin or gum.

expatiate, spread out. (L. *spatior*, walk abroad.)

confer, discuss.

776. straitened, crowded close together for want of space. (Strait = narrow.)

779. Cp. 428 and 429.

780. pygmean race. See 575 *n.*

781. Indian mount, the Himalayas.

faery elves, fairy sprites or spirits. The modern use *fairy* is incorrect: it is, properly, an adjective, as here—*fay-like.* So in *Comus,* "faery vision". (*Fay,* Low L. *fata,* a fate, a fay.)

783. belated, kept late. Cp. benighted, overtaken by the fall of night.

785. arbitress, witness, spectator. (L. *arbiter,* umpire, witness.)

nearer to the earth. Fairies, witches, &c., were supposed to be able to draw the moon down towards the earth by their enchantments.

786. pale. What does this word qualify? What is the figure? Cp. *Il Penseroso,* 67-69, where Milton speaks of the moon "wandering as if led astray".

788. with joy and fear : explain.

790. were at large, had plenty of room.

792. infernal : see 241 *n.*

795. close : cp. 646.

recess, retirement, or, a retired place.

conclave, assembly. This is the name specially applied to the secret meeting of cardinals at Rome when a pope is to be elected. (G.)

797. frequent, numerous, crowded (L. *frequens*); qualifying *conclave.*

798. consult, consultation. (L. *consultum,* a consultation or decree, especially of the senate or chief council.)

TABLE OF DEITIES MENTIONED IN LL. 392-521.

Lines.	Deities.	By whom Worshipped.	Character.	Scripture References.
392-405	MOLOCH.	(1) The Ammonites. (2) The Jews at Jerusalem.	A fire or sun god; supposed to be able to ward off the destructive heat of the sun.	Lev. xviii. 21. Ps. cvi. 37, 38. Jer. vii. 31.
406-418	CHEMOS.	(1) The Moabites and Seon[1] their invader. The places mentioned in 407-11 all lie east of the Dead Sea, between Mt. Nebo in the north and R. Arnon in the south. (2) The Jews at the hill Peor (hence the plague[2]) and at Jerusalem.	Like Moloch.	2 Ki. iii. 27; and xxiii. 13. [1] Num. xxi. 26. [2] Num. xxv. 2, 3, 9.
419-446	BAALIM and ASHTEROTH.	(1) The various Phœnician and Canaanitish nations from north (*Euphrates*) to south (*brook Besor*). (2) The Jews at Jerusalem.	These were national and other forms of Moloch.	1 Kings xi. 5. Judg. ii. 13. Gen. xv. 18.
446-457	THAMMUZ.	The Syrians, Jews[3], Egyptians, &c.	A legendary Phœnician prince killed by a boar near the river Adonis in Lebanon. The colouring of the stream in the spring floods gave rise to the legend of his 'annual wound'.	[3] Ezek. viii. 14.

TABLE OF DEITIES—*Continued.*

Lines.	Deities.	By whom Worshipped.	Character.	Scripture References.
457–466	DAGON.	The Philistines (Azotus = Ashdod; Accaron = Ekron).	Fish (?) and corn god. Had the face and hands of a man, and the tail of a fish.	For the allusion see 1 Sam. v. 4: "Dagon was fallen to the ground . . . and the head and the palms were cut off upon the threshold".
467–476	RIMMON.	The Syrians (at Damascus).		Naaman, a Syrian leper, when cured by Elisha, forsook Rimmon (2 Ki. v.). Later, Ahaz, king of Judah, set up a Syrian altar (2 Kings xvi.).
476–489	OSIRIS, ISIS, and ORUS.	The Egyptians.	*Osiris* ('the Good'), *Isis*, his consort, and *Orus*, their son. Osiris has another son, Typhon ('evil'), with whom he is ever in conflict, but, through the help of Isis and Orus, is never overcome. Osiris was worshipped under the form of a bull (Apis); Isis, of a woman with cow's horns.	
490–505	[BELIAL (Hebrew, wickedness, worthlessness), not a god, but a personification of evil.]		Whereas the deities are identified with open, acknowledged wickedness, 'Belial' is used by Milton to symbolise the evil that is secret, or disguised under the cloak of religion, wealth, or rank.	

TABLE OF DEITIES—*Continued.*

Lines.	Deities.	By whom Worshipped.	
506–521	The Ionian (or Grecian) deities, sprung from Uranus and Ge (198 *n.*), Heaven and Earth Kronos or Saturn and Rhea } and ten other Titans The Giants. Jove.	The Greeks ('Javan's issue') — in Crete, on Olympus, at Delphi and Dodona, &c. — Romans, Gauls, and Celts.	

DEFINITIONS, WITH EXAMPLES,

OF THE CHIEF FIGURES OF SPEECH OCCURRING IN BOOK I.

1. ALLITERATION: the rhythmical repetition of a sound in poetry.
"Deep in a dungeon was the captive cast,
Deprived of day and held in fetters fast." Dryden.
See l. 768.

2. ANAKOLU'THON, or non-sequence: a sudden change in the form of a passage. See lines 84, 623, &c.

3. ANTITHESIS: the contrasting of opposite notions. (Cp. No. 12.)
"From toil he wins his spirit's light,
From busy day the peaceful night." Gray.

4. CHIA'SMUS: arranging corresponding terms symmetrically, or cross-wise, like the letter X. (Gk. 'chi'.)
        a   b   b   a
"Shallow brooks and rivers wide."

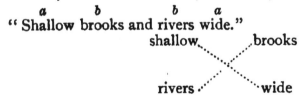

5. EUPHEMISM: the use of a pleasant or mild term instead of one that is disagreeable or strong. See lines 623 and 624.
Irony is one form of this. See 318.

6. HENDI'ADYS: the use of two nouns instead of a noun and an adjective. (Gk. 'one thing through two'.)
"Among sweet dews and flowers." Milton.
(*i.e.* sweet dewy flowers.)

7. HYPA'LLAGE': transferring an adjective to a word to which it does not properly refer. (Gk. 'an interchange'.) *E.g.* 'The wisest heart of Solomon' (l. 400). A special case of Hypallage is *Prolepsis*—the use of a word by anticipation.

8. HYPERBOLE: exaggeration. (Gk. 'a throwing beyond the mark'.) See ll. 633, and 655-56.

9. METAPHOR: a transference of qualities or actions from one thing to another.
"Be he the fire, I'll be the yielding water." Shakespeare.
See l. 294. (Milton is very sparing in the use of metaphor, but he excels in his use of simile.)

10. METON'YMY: naming a thing by some accompaniment or connection. (Gk. 'a change of name'.) (Cp. No. 17.)
"The pen is mightier than the sword."
"I am reading Milton."

11. ONOMATOPŒ'IA: imitating the sense by the sound of the words used.
"The deep-domed Empyrëan
Rings to the roar of an angel-onset." Tennyson.
And "The brooks of Eden mazily murmuring". Tennyson.
Cp. ll. 668 and 768.

12. OXYMO'RON: placing together words of opposed meanings. (Cp. No. 3.) (Gk. 'an apparent contradiction'.)
"With wanton heed and giddy cunning." Milton.
See ll. 63 and 692.

13. PARONOMA'SIA: placing together words of similar sound. See ll. 606 and 642.

14. PERSONIFICATION: attributing to inanimate objects qualities or actions peculiar to living beings. See ll. 490 ('Belial'), 601-2, 574-75, &c.

15. PLEONASM: the use of superfluous words. (Gk. 'fulness'.)
"Encompassed round with foes." Milton.
See ll. 2-3, 13-14, 281, &c.

16. SIMILE: a comparison, usually limited to one point. See ll. 302, 591, 745, &c.

17. SYNEC'DOCHE': putting the name of a part for that of the whole, of the material for the complete thing, &c. (Cp. No. 10.)
"To bless the doors from nightly harm." Milton.
See ll. 519, 563, 739, &c.

18. ZEUGMA: the construction in which two (or more) words depend on another word which suits only one of them, but suggests an appropriate word for the other. (Gk. 'a yoking together'.)
"To the silvan lodge they came,
With flowerets decked and fragrant smells." Milton.

Of the above, Nos. 1, 2, 4, 11, and 13 are mere mechanical devices, not figures of speech, though, for convenience, usually included under this term.

---

19. DOUBLETS: words differing in form, but etymologically one and the same. *E.g.* Benison and benediction; extraneous and strange; paralysis and palsy.

20. HOMONYMS: words which are spelt alike, but differ considerably in meaning. E.g. *spell*, an incantation, a thin slip of wood, a turn of work, to tell the names of letters. So beetle, lay, &c.

21. SYNONYMS: words having nearly the same meaning. *E.g.* Begin and commence; idle and lazy; slothful and indolent.

22. HYBRID: a word that is made up from two (or more) different languages: as *bankrupt—bank* being a Teutonic word, whilst *-rupt* is from the Latin. Cp. interwove, architrave, &c.

EXTRA NOTES, MOSTLY ETYMOLOGICAL.

ambitious (41), aspiring: originally, *ambitio* was the *going about* of candidates for office at Rome seeking votes; canvassing. (L. *ambi*, and *itum*, to go.)

Archangel (600), lit. chief angel or messenger. (Gk.) Cp. **architect** (732), chief builder.

conclave (795), originally a locked-up place. (L. *clavis*, a key.)

disastrous (597), unfavourable. In the language of Astrology, a *disaster* was due to the *stars*. (Gk. *astron*, a star.) So 'influence' denoted the power which stars exerted on human affairs, 'that which *flowed* upon us'. A *jovial* person was 'born under' Jove, and was therefore of a cheerful disposition.

ensign (536), a standard. (L. *insignis*, remarkable; from *in*, and *signum*, a mark: hence 'having a mark on it'. Skeat.)

entrance (301), to put into a trance or swoon, to cause to become unconscious. (L. *transitus*, a passing away or across.)

homicide (417), deadly, murderous. (L. *homo*, and *caedo*, kill: cp. fratricide, &c.)

legion (632), a large body of soldiers. A Roman legion consisted of from 4200 to 6000 men.

magic (727), lit. the science of the *magi*, wise men who interpreted dreams among the Persians.

meteor (537), a conspicuous fiery body in the sky. (Gk. 'something raised aloft'.)

mood (in *Dorian Mood*, 550), denotes the character of the music—grave, soothing, stirring, &c., and this depended mainly on

F

the arrangement of the intervals.   We now use the term *mode* (as ' minor mode ').

myriad (622), ' ten thousand '.   (Gk.)

opprobrious (403), full of reproach.   (L. *opprobrium*, disgrace.)

oracle (12), a divine utterance; here the place where such utterances are delivered.

orgies (415), wild revelry and excesses.   (L. *orgia*, a festival in honour of Bacchus : Gk. *orgé*, wild emotion or passion.)

rhime (16), verse or poetry; from the numerical regularity of the lines.   A.S. *rím*, number.   Hence the correct form is *rime* : the intrusion of the letter *h* is due to confusion with *rhythm*.

shrine (388), altar : also a costly elaborate tomb; or a place where relics are deposited.   (L. *scrinium*, a chest.)

wanton (414), unrestrained, wild.   (O.E. *wan*, lacking, and *teón*, draw, educate.)

SYNOPTICAL TABLES.

I. Scriptural Names.

(a) *Persons.*

307.	Busiris.
339.	Amram's son.
396.	Ammonite.
342.	Pharaoh.
401. 444.	Solomon.
406.	Moab.
409.	Seon.
418.	Josiah.
455.	Ezekiel.
472.	Ahaz.
495.	Eli's sons.

(b) *Places.*

4.	Eden.
7. 484.	Oreb. Sinai.
10.	Sion hill.
11.	Siloa's brook.
307.	Memphian (chivalry).
309.	Goshen.
397-9.	Rabba, Argob, Basan, Arnon.
404-5.	Hinnom, Tophet, Gehenna.
407.	Aroer, Nebo.
408-9.	Abarim, Hesebon, Horonaim.
410.	Sibma.
411.	Elealè. Asphaltic pool.
413.	Sittim.
420.	Euphrates.
421. 448.	Syria.
438.	Phoenicians.
441.	Sidonian (virgins).
443.	Mount of Olives (' that offensive mtn.', &c.),
447.	Lebanon.
450.	Adonis.
457.	Judah.
464-6.	Azotus, Gath, Ascalon, Accaron, and Gaza.
468-9.	Damascus, Abana, and Pharphar.
485.	Bethel and Dan.
503.	Sodom.
504.	Gibeah.
694.	Babel.
717.	Babylon.

II. CLASSICAL NAMES.

(a) *Deities, &c.*

198. Titanian.
    Earth-born.
198. } Jove.
512. }
199. Briareos.
    Typhon.
508. Ionian gods.
510. Titan.
513. Rhea.

(b) *Places.*

15. Aonian mt.
200. Tarsus.
232. Pelorus.
233. Ætna.

508. Ionian (gods).
514-5. Crete and Ida.
516. Olympus.
517. Delphi.
518. Dodona.
519. } Doric land.
550. } Dorian mood.
714. } Doric pillars.
520. } Adria, and Hesperian fields.
577. Phlegra.
578. Thebes and Ilium.
694. Babel and Memphian.
717. Babylon and Alcairo.
721. Assyria.
739. Ausonian land.
746. Lemnos.

III. MISCELLANEOUS NAMES.

288. Tuscan artist.
289. Fesolè.
290. Valdarno.
303. Vallombrosa.
    Etruria.
353. Rhene, Danaw.
355. Libyan sands.
580. Uther's son.
581. Armoric knights.

583. Aspramont.
    Montalban.
584. Damasco.
    Marocco.
    Trebisond.
585. Biserta.
586. Charlemain.
587. Fontarabbia.

SOME PARALLEL PASSAGES FROM THE CLASSICS.

84. " O how fallen! how changed ", &c.

Cp. Virgil, *Aeneid*, ii. 274—

" Heu mihi, qualis erat! quantum mutatus ab illo!"

94. " Yet not for those .....do I repent ", &c.

Cp. Æschylus, *Prometheus*, 991—

" Let his gleaming flame be hurled......for none of these things shall bend me."

98.   " High disdain from sense of injured merit."

Cp. Virgil, *Aeneid*, i. 27—

" Manet alta mente repostum
Judicium Paridis spretaeque injuriae formae."

171.   " The sulphurous hail
Shot after us in storm, o'erblown, hath laid
The fiery surge."

Storr compares Sophocles, *Ajax*, 674—

" The blowing of fierce winds leaves the moaning sea asleep."

253.   "A mind not to be changed by place or time."

Cp. Horace, *Epistles*, i. xi. 27—

" Caelum non animum mutant qui trans mare currunt."

619.   " Thrice he essayed, and thrice", &c.

Cp. Ovid, *Metamorphoses*, xi. 419—

" Ter conata loqui, ter fletibus ora rigavit."

623.   " And that strife
Was not inglorious", &c.

Cp. Ovid, *Metamorphoses*, ix. 6—

" Nec tam
Turpe fuit vinci quam contendesse decorum est."

742.   " From morn
To noon he fell, from noon to dewy eve", &c.

Beeching compares *Iliad*, i. 591, where Hephæstus says—

" He caught me by my foot, and hurled me from the heavenly
threshold; all day I flew, and at the set of sun I fell in
Lemnos."

LIST OF PASSAGES FOR PARAPHRASING.

LIST OF PASSAGES FOR COMMITTING TO MEMORY.

LINES

1. Nine times the space .... sulphur unconsumed; 50–69.
2. If thou beest he .... shook his throne; 84–105.
3. What though the................ of heaven; 105–124.
4. Fallen Cherub.................... from our foe; 157–179.
5. Thus Satan .... the burning lake; 192–210.
6. Forthwith upright .... supernal power; 221–241.
7. He scarce had .... overarched imbower; 283–304.
8. That proud honour............. immortal minds; 533–559.
9. Thus far these .... waiting revenge; 587–604.
10. Cruel his eye..................... their way; 604–621.
11. O myriads .... wrought our fall; 622–642.
12. Henceforth his.................. vault or heaven; 643–669.
13. Anon, out of.................... as from a sky; 710–730.
14. The hasty multitude .... build in hell; 730–751.
15. As bees............................ heart rebounds; 768–788.

LIST OF PASSAGES FOR ANALYSIS.

1. Of man's first .... out of Chaos; 1–10.
2. Or, if Sion hill .... prose or rhime; 10–16.
3. He it was.......................... if he opposed; 34–41.
4. Yet not for those................ and shook his throne; 94–105.
5. O Prince! O chief .... in endless misery; 128–142.
6. But what if he.................... the gloomy deep; 143–152.
7. To be weak .... whom we resist; 157–162.
8. If then his providence .... their destined aim; 162–168.
9. Thither let us tend .... from despair; 183–191.
10. His other parts .... morn delays; 194–208.
11. So stretched out .... and vengeance poured; 209–220.
12. Then with expanded .... stench and smoke; 225–237.
13. Be it so .... above his equals; 245–249.
14. If once they hear .... astounded and amazed; 274–281.
15. Nathless he so................... chariot wheels; 299–311.
16. They heard and were .... well awake; 331–334.
17. As when the .... all the plain; 338–350.
18. The chief were those .... affront his light; 381–391.
19. Next came one .... his worshippers; 457–461.
20. For never, since................. by Fontarabbia; 573–587.
21. As when the sun .... the Archangel; 594–600.
22. Yet faithful how .... the blasted heath; 611–615.
23. That strife .... their native seat; 623–634.
24. But he who reigns .... wrought our fall; 636–642.
25. Our better part .... half his foe; 645–649.
26. And here let .... scarce perform; 692–699.
27. His hand was .... orders bright; 732–737.
28. As bees .... behold a wonder; 768–777.
29. They but now .... her pale course; 777–786.

LIST OF WORDS EXPLAINED IN THE NOTES.

(For words marked G. see p. 81.)

rased, 362
recorders, 551
reign, 543
religious, 372
remorse, 605
reprobate, 697
rhime, 12. G.
rife, 650
rites, 414
rout, 747

satiate, 179
scathed, 613
scummed, 704
secure, 261
serried, 548

shrine, 388. G.
skiff, 204
sluiced, 702
sovran, 753
straitened, 776
study, 107
Stygian, 239 ·
sublimed, 235
sultan, 348
supernal, 241
suppliant, 112
swage, 556

temper, 285. G.
thralls, 149
timbrels, 394

touches, 557
trophies, 539
tyranny, 124

urge, 68
utter, 72

various, 706
vaunting, 126

wanton, 414. G.
warping, 341
weltering, 78
witnessed, 57
wont, 764

zenith, 745

BLACKIE AND SON'S
Educational Catalogue.

ELEMENTARY CLASSICS.

Caesar's Gallic War. BOOK I. Edited, with Introduction, Notes, Exercises, and Vocabularies, by JOHN BROWN, B.A., Worcester College, Oxford; Assistant to the Professor of Humanity in Glasgow University. With coloured map, pictorial illustrations, and plans of battles. F'cap 8vo, cloth, 1s. 6d.

"Well printed, with short and, so far as we have tested them, accurate notes. The introduction contains some useful drawings illustrating Roman military life, and there is a map of Gaul so cunningly pasted into the cover that it can be kept open for reference without trailing clumsily about, no matter what part of the book is being read."—Journal of Education.

Caesar's Gallic War. BOOK II. Edited on the same plan by JOHN BROWN, B.A. F'cap 8vo, cloth, 1s. 6d.

"In noticing Mr. Brown's edition of Book I. we stated that it was one of the most complete text-books we had seen: the same remark applies to this volume. We cannot speak too highly of Mr. Brown's careful and scholarly workmanship." —School Guardian.

"The best school edition of Caesar we know."—Academic Review.

Caesar's Invasions of Britain. (Parts of Books IV. and V. of the Gallic War.) Edited by JOHN BROWN, B.A. F'cap 8vo, cloth, 1s. 6d.

Virgil's Aeneid. BOOK I. Edited, with Introduction, Outline of Prosody, Notes, Exercises on the Hexameter, Vocabulary, &c., by REV. A. J. CHURCH, M.A., sometime Professor of Latin in University College, London. F'cap 8vo, cloth, 1s.

"The little manual is admirable, not only in its critical introduction and sensible notes, but in its comprehension of the real and not the imaginary stumbling-blocks which confront the beginner."—Speaker.

Ovid. Selections in Elegiac and Hexameter Verse. Edited, with Introduction, Notes, and Vocabulary, by A. H. ALLCROFT, M.A., Christ Church, Oxford. F'cap 8vo, cloth, 1s. 6d.

Phaedrus' Fables. BOOKS I. AND II. Edited for junior forms, by S. E. WINBOLT, B.A., Assistant Master in Christ's Hospital. F'cap 8vo, cloth, 1s.

ELEMENTARY CLASSICS—*Continued.*

Latin Stories: Short selections from the best prose authors. Edited with Notes, English Exercises, Vocabularies, and an Introductory Note on Translation, by A. D. GODLEY, M.A., Fellow and Tutor of Magdalen College, Oxford. F'cap 8vo, cloth, 1s.

"A little book nicely done. The length of each story is about equal to that which would be set for one lesson—a praiseworthy feature. . . . Altogether this is a very useful little book."—Educational Review.

Latin Unseens: graduated specimens of prose and verse, suitable for practice in unseen translation, and mainly selected from Examination Papers. Junior Section. Paper covers, 32 pp., price 3d.
[*Middle and Senior Sections preparing.*

Praxis Primaria: Exercises in Latin Composition. By the Rev. ISLAY BURNS, M.A., D.D. Seventh Edition, crown 8vo, cloth limp, 2s. KEY, 3s. 6d.

Xenophon's Anabasis. BOOK I. Edited, with Introduction, Notes, an Appendix on Greek Constructions, and Vocabulary, by C. E. BROWNRIGG, M.A., Chief Classical Master in Magdalen College School, Oxford. With Map, Plans of Battles, &c. F'cap 8vo, cloth, 1s. 6d.

"The schoolmaster who uses this book as its editor intends, and secures the attention of his pupils to its contents, will not fail to impart a fair knowledge of an excellent Greek text, and must excite in the minds of the best boys a love of Greek which will charm them on to further reaches of reading and research."—Educational News.

HIGHER CLASSICS.

Horace's Historical and Political Odes. Edited, with Historical Introduction and Notes, by the Rev. A. J. CHURCH, M.A., sometime Professor of Latin at University College, London. Crown 8vo, cloth, 2s. 6d.

Silver Age Prose: Selections from Latin of the Silver Age. Edited by C. E. BROWNRIGG, M.A., Chief Classical Master in Magdalen College School, Oxford. With an Introduction by T. H. WARREN, M.A., President of Magdalen College. Crown 8vo, cloth.
[*Nearly ready.*

A Classical Compendium: being a Handbook to Greek and Latin Constructions. By C. E. BROWNRIGG, M.A., Chief Classical Master in Magdalen College School, Oxford. Crown 8vo, cloth, 2s. 6d.

"An excellent handbook. The author's scholarship is good, and his grammar up to date; his facts are well arranged, and the parallelisms between Greek and Latin kept constantly in view. We confidently recommend the book to students for University classical entrance scholarships, and all higher classical examinations."—University Correspondent.

Myths and Legends of Greece and Rome. A Handbook of Mythology. By E. M. BERENS. Illustrated. *New Edition.* F'cap 8vo, cloth, 2s. 6d.

ENGLISH LITERATURE.

THE WARWICK LIBRARY.

A series of Comparative Manuals of English Literature. Crown 8vo, cloth.

General Editor—Professor C. H. HERFORD, Litt.D.

Pastoral Poetry. With an Introduction by E. K. CHAMBERS, M.A.
[In the press.

Literary Criticism. With an Introduction by C. E. VAUGHAN, M.A.
[In preparation.

English Letter-Writers. With an Introduction by W. RALEIGH, M.A.
[In preparation.

Tales in Verse. With an Introduction by C. H. HERFORD, Litt.D.
[In preparation.

Other volumes to follow.

The Warwick Shakespeare: A new series of the greater Plays, suitable for students of literature and senior candidates in the University Local Examinations.

AS YOU LIKE IT.—Edited by J. C. SMITH, M.A., Lecturer in Owens College, and sometime exhibitioner of Trinity College, Oxford. F'cap 8vo, cloth, 1s. 6d.

HAMLET.—Edited by E. K. CHAMBERS, B.A., sometime Scholar of Corpus Christi College, Oxford. F'cap 8vo, cloth, 1s. 6d.
"In an excellent series, this play seems to be specially well edited. . . . Its appendices will give an intelligent student more than an inkling of what literature, literary history, and literary criticism mean."—Bookman.

MACBETH.—Edited by the same. F'cap 8vo, cloth, 1s.
"His remarks on the unities of action, thought, atmosphere, and structure in *Macbeth* display a keen insight into the beauties and lessons of the tragedy. The notes are particularly clear, and the seven appendices will well repay the careful attention of any Shakespearean student."—School Guardian.

RICHARD II.—Edited by C. H. HERFORD, Litt.D., Professor of English at University College, Aberystwyth. F'cap 8vo, cloth, 1s. 6d.
"What we wanted and what we now have is interpretation of character, of motive, of action. Here is a book which will help the student to appreciate the spirit of the drama, and the relation of the drama to life. The really important philological difficulties are tersely dealt with."—Educational Review.

JULIUS CÆSAR.—Edited by A. D. INNES, M.A., sometime Scholar of Oriel College, Oxford. F'cap 8vo, cloth, 1s.
"We have encountered few better works of the kind, and we heartily commend them, on the score of common sense as well as scholarship, to teachers and private students."—The Speaker.

In Preparation.

RICHARD THE THIRD.—Edited by GEO. MACDONALD, M.A., Balliol College, Oxford.

THE MERCHANT OF VENICE.—Edited by H. L. WITHERS, B.A., Principal of Borough Road Training College.

THE TEMPEST.—Edited by F. S. BOAS, M.A., Balliol College, Oxford.

CYMBELINE.—Edited by A. J. WYATT, M.A., Christ's College, Cambridge.

TWELFTH NIGHT.—Edited by A. D. INNES, M.A., Oriel College, Oxford.

KING LEAR.—Edited by W. H. LOW, M.A., Trinity College, Cambridge.

HENRY THE FIFTH.—Edited by G. C. MOORE SMITH, M.A., St. John's College, Cambridge.

ENGLISH LITERATURE—*Continued.*

Introduction to Shakespeare. By Professor DOWDEN. Illustrated. Crown 8vo, cloth, 2s. 6d.

"Mr. Dowden's book will be most valuable by way of biography, while his criticisms have all the sanity and insight which we expect from him. The little book is singularly complete; it sketches the history of Shakespearean editorship and criticism and acting, and is full of help to students in their novitiate."—**Daily Chronicle.**

Blackie's Junior School Shakespeare: A new series, designed specially for young students, and suitable for junior candidates in the University Local Examinations, &c.

HAMLET.—Edited by L. W. LYDE, M.A., Chief English Master in Glasgow Academy. Cloth, 10d.

KING JOHN.—Edited by F. E. WEBB, B.A., sometime Scholar of Queen's College, Oxford. Cloth, 8d.

THE TEMPEST. Edited by ELIZABETH LEE, Lecturer in English Literature, Streatham Hill High School for Girls. Cloth, 8d.

THE MERCHANT OF VENICE.—Edited by GEORGE H. ELY, B.A., sometime Assistant Master in the United Westminster Schools. Cloth, 8d.

"Good and cheap."—**University Correspondent.**

HENRY THE EIGHTH.—Edited by the same. Cloth, 8d.

"In every respect the little book is the ideal of what a school Shakespeare should be."—**Glasgow Herald.**

HENRY THE FIFTH.—Edited by W. BARRY, B.A., English Master at Tettenhall College, Staffordshire. Cloth, 8d.

"Well bound, clearly printed, and judiciously edited, it is admirably adapted to the use of junior forms."—**School Guardian.**

RICHARD THE SECOND.—Edited by the same. Cloth, 8d.

CORIOLANUS.—Edited by WALTER DENT. Cloth, 10d.

"We commend this edition to the favourable regard of teachers as a piece of good, intelligent work."—**Educational News.**

JULIUS CÆSAR.—Edited by the same. Cloth, 8d.

"An excellent edition. There is more explanatory paraphrasing and less verbal exposition in this edition than in most others. The introduction is informing, not controversial, and the apparatus in the notes and index is just of the sort that will be helpful to young students."—**Educational News.**

AS YOU LIKE IT.—Edited by LIONEL W. LYDE, M.A., Queen's College, Oxford; Head English Master, Glasgow Academy. Cloth, 8d.

"A model of what a book intended for the local examinations ought to be."—**Daily Mail.**

A MIDSUMMER-NIGHT'S DREAM.—Edited by W. F. BAUGUST, Chief Master of Modern Subjects in the United Westminster Schools. Cloth, 8d.

In Preparation.

RICHARD THE THIRD.—Edited by F. E. WEBB, B.A., Editor of *King John.*

TWELFTH NIGHT.—Edited by ELIZABETH LEE, Editor of *The Tempest.*

CYMBELINE.—Edited by W. F. BAUGUST, Editor of *A Midsummer-Night's Dream.*

MACBETH.—Edited by H. J. NOTCUTT, B.A., Second Master in Battersea Grammar School.

BLACKIE'S ENGLISH CLASSICS.

Milton's Paradise Lost. BOOK I. Edited especially for junior students by F. GORSE, M.A., Second Master in Parmiter's School, Victoria Park. F'cap 8vo, cloth, 1s. [*Nearly ready.*]

Macaulay's Essay on Addison. Edited by C. SHELDON, D.Lit., M.A., Headmaster of the English Department, Royal Academical Institution, Belfast. F'cap 8vo, cloth, 2s.

"The introduction is on right lines, and includes nothing superfluous. . . . The notes are business-like, scholarly, and not—as is too often the case—gratuitously learned."—*Journal of Education.*

Carlyle. Readings from Carlyle. With Introduction and Notes by W. KEITH LEASK, M.A., late Scholar of Worcester College, Oxford. Crown 8vo, cloth, 2s. 6d.

"An excellent introduction to the study of Carlyle."—*Globe.*

Wordsworth: Selections from the Shorter Poems. Edited by WALTER DENT. Paper, 2d.; cloth, 3d.

Addison's Sir Roger de Coverley. Edited by FRANCES E. WILCROFT. F'cap 8vo, cloth, 10d.

"A capital little prose classic. . . . The author has prefaced her selections with a brightly written life of Addison; the notes are remarkably well selected and judiciously treated."—*Guardian.*

Coleridge's Ancient Mariner. Edited by W. DENT, editor of *Coriolanus*, &c. Paper, 2d.; cloth, 3d.

Goldsmith: The Good-natured Man. With Notes. Edited by HAROLD LITTLEDALE, M.A., Senior Moderator, Trin. Coll., Dublin; Fellow of the University of Bombay; Vice-principal of H. H. Gaekwar's College and High School, Baroda. Cloth, 10d.

"Very few, if any, real difficulties are passed over without satisfactory solution, the historical and other allusions being fully and correctly given."—*Athenæum.*

Goldsmith: She Stoops to Conquer. Edited by HAROLD LITTLEDALE, M.A. With Notes. F'cap 8vo, cloth, 10d.

Goldsmith's Deserted Village. Edited by ELIZABETH LEE, editor of *The Tempest*, &c. Paper, 2d.; cloth, 3d.

Gray's Elegy, Eton College Ode, and The Bard. Edited by ELIZABETH LEE, Lecturer in English at Streatham Hill High School. Paper, 2d.; cloth, 3d.

Macaulay's Battle of the Lake Regillus. With Introduction and Notes. Paper, 2d.; cloth, 3d.

Macaulay's Horatius, and Battle of the Lake Regillus. With Introduction and Notes. In one volume, cloth, 6d.

Macaulay's Horatius. With Introduction and Notes. Paper, 2d.; cloth, 3d.

ENGLISH CLASSICS—*Continued.*

Macaulay's Armada, Ivry, and Battle of Naseby. With Introductions and Notes. Paper, 2*d.*; cloth, 3*d.*

Scott's Lay of the Last Minstrel. Complete, with Introduction and Notes. F'cap 8vo, cloth, 1*s.* 6*d.* Also in Two Parts, Cantos I.–III., cloth, 10*d.*; and IV.–VI., cloth, 1*s.* And in single cantos, paper, 2*d.* each; cloth, 3*d.* each.

"As a help to literary appreciation of the poem by young students this edition merits the highest praise. The notes contain nothing we could well spare, and the introduction is as valuable as the notes."—**University Correspondent.**

Shakespeare: Selections from As You Like It. With the Story of the play and Notes. Paper, 2*d.*; cloth, 3*d.*

Selections from Standard Authors, with Introductions and Simple Notes. Each 32 pp., paper, 2*d.*; cloth, 3*d.*

SHAKESPEARE: MERCHANT OF VENICE, Acts I. III. and IV.

SHAKESPEARE: SELECTIONS FROM HENRY VIII. and JULIUS CÆSAR.

SHAKESPEARE: SELECTIONS FROM RICHARD II. and HENRY IV., Part II.

BACON'S ESSAYS (Selections from).

MILTON: L'ALLEGRO and IL PENSEROSO.

GOLDSMITH: TRAVELLER.

BURNS: COTTER'S SATURDAY NIGHT, &c.

BYRON: PROPHECY OF DANTE. CANTOS I. and II.

BYRON: PRISONER OF CHILLON.

MOORE: FIRE WORSHIPPERS. Parts I. and II.

CRABBE: THE VILLAGE.

SCOTT: LADY OF THE LAKE. CANTO I., THE CHASE. CANTO V., THE COMBAT.

SCOTT: MARMION, CANTO VI.

CAMPBELL: THE PLEASURES OF HOPE. Part I.

HOGG: THE QUEEN'S WAKE.

MACAULAY: ESSAY ON BUNYAN.

LONGFELLOW: EVANGELINE (64 pp., paper, 3*d.*; cloth, 4*d.*).

The Pupil's English Grammar: An Introduction to the study of English Grammar, based upon the Analysis of Sentences. Cloth boards, 1*s.* 6*d.*

"A very young child may be made to understand what a sentence is, and to break it up into subject and predicate. When once the foundation is laid, the meaning of noun and verb will naturally follow, and a knowledge of adjective, adverb, and the other parts of speech may be safely superimposed. This is the method which has been consistently followed in *The Pupil's English Grammar*, which we recommend."—**Daily Chronicle.**

Handbook of English Composition Exercises. Comprising Short Stories, Subjects, and Hints for Essays, Rules and Models for Letters, &c. F'cap 8vo, cloth, 1*s.*

Stories and Essays: A Series of Exercises in English Composition. Carefully arranged and graduated Stories for Exercises, and a number of classified Examples for Essays. F'cap 8vo, cloth, 1*s.*

Baynham's Elocution: Selections from leading Authors and Dramatists. With Rules and Instructions and carefully graduated Exercises. By GEO. W. BAYNHAM. *Seventh Edition,* revised and extended. 448 pp., crown 8vo, cloth, 2*s.* 6*d.*

MODERN LANGUAGES.

MODERN FRENCH TEXTS.

Edited by FRANCIS STORR, B.A., Chief Master of the Modern Side, Merchant Taylors' School.

Lettres de Paul-Louis Courier. Edited by J. G. ANDERSON, B.A., Lond., Prizeman in French; French Master at Merchant Taylors' School. F'cap 8vo, cloth, 1s.

The Court of Spain under Charles II., and other Historical Essays by SAINT-VICTOR. Edited by F. STORR. F'cap 8vo, cloth, 1s.

Voyages en Zigzag. By RODOLPHE TÖPFFER. Edited by R. HOPE MONCRIEFF. F'cap 8vo, cloth, 1s. *[In the press.*

BLACKIE'S MODERN LANGUAGE SERIES.

Fleur de Mer. By PIERRE MAËL. Edited by J. BOIELLE, B.ès-L. F'cap 8vo, cloth, 1s.

French Stories: A Reading-book for Junior and Middle Forms. With Notes, English Exercises, and Vocabulary, by MARGUERITE NINET, French Mistress at the Girls' High School, Graham Street, Eaton Square, London. F'cap 8vo, cloth, 1s.

"The work is skilfully done."—Journal of Education.

"The authoress has succeeded in making the whole lively, bright, and interesting. The work will be found a capital little reading book for lower and middle forms."—Educational News.

Readings in French: a companion volume to *French Stories*. By MARGUERITE NINET. F'cap 8vo, cloth, 1s. 6d.

A Modern French Reader: Interesting extracts from contemporary French. With Notes and Vocabulary by J. J. BEUZEMAKER, B.A., Examiner to the College of Preceptors, &c. F'cap 8vo, cloth, 1s.

"The editor has succeeded in his aim, not to have a dull page in the book. The pieces chosen are chiefly narrative; they are sometimes descriptive; but all have brightness, and sparkle and point, and are frequently full of humour."—Academic Review.

French Unseens. Passages in Prose and Verse. Uniform with *Latin Unseens*. Paper, 3d.

Schiller's Song of the Bell, and other Poems. Edited by GEORGE MACDONALD, M.A., Balliol College, Oxford. Crown 8vo, cloth, 8d.

"This may well be termed an *édition de luxe*. Type and paper are luxurious, and the marginal analysis which accompanies the text will prove a welcome luxury, a clue to the chief difficulty of the poem, which lies in the connection of ideas. The notes are plain and sensible."—Journal of Education.

"A very pleasant, useful, and cheap little volume."—University Correspondent.

HISTORY.

THE OXFORD MANUALS OF ENGLISH HISTORY.

Edited by C. W. C. OMAN, M.A., Fellow of All Souls College, Oxford. In f'cap 8vo volumes, with maps, &c.; neat cloth, 1s.

I. **The Making of the English Nation,** B.C. 55–A.D. 1135. By C. G. ROBERTSON, B.A., Fellow of All Souls College. [*Ready.*

II. **The Early Plantagenets,** A.D. 1135–1328. By W. H. HUTTON, M.A., Fellow and Tutor of St. John's College. [*In preparation.*

III. **The Hundred Years' War,** A.D. 1328–1485. By C. W. C. OMAN, M.A., Editor of the Series. [*In preparation.*

IV. **England and the Reformation,** A.D. 1485–1603. By G. W. POWERS, M.A., formerly Scholar of New College. [*In preparation.*

V. **King and Parliament,** A.D. 1603–1714. By G. H. WAKELING, M.A., Lecturer in History at Wadham College. [*Ready.*

VI. **The Making of the British Empire,** A.D. 1714–1832. By ARTHUR HASSALL, M.A., Senior Student and Tutor of Christ Church. [*In preparation.*

A Summary of British History. With Appendices. By the Rev. EDGAR SANDERSON, M.A., sometime Scholar of Clare College, Cambridge; author of "A History of the British Empire", &c., 208 pp., crown 8vo, cloth, 1s.

"Considering its size and price, this *Summary* contains a marvellous amount of information; and, what is very important, it carries the student right on to the present year."—**University Correspondent.**

"A remarkably good condensation: it would be difficult to name any book where the student who wishes to get up either British history as a whole or any particular period could find the information better put for examination purposes."—**Glasgow Herald.**

A History of the British Empire. With Pictorial Illustrations, Tables, Maps, and Plans. By the Rev. EDGAR SANDERSON, M.A. 476 pp., cloth, 2s. 6d.

"A capital school history. The narrative is comprehensive and well condensed, while the auxiliary apparatus of tables and dates and marginal references is put together with a good regard to the needs of a young student."—**Scotsman.**

Outlines of the World's History, ANCIENT, MEDIÆVAL, and MODERN, with special relation to the History of Civilization and the Progress of Mankind. By the Rev. EDGAR SANDERSON, M.A., sometime Scholar of Clare College, Cambridge. With many Illustrations and Coloured Maps. 664 pp., crown 8vo, cloth, red edges, 6s. 6d.

Also separately:—Part I., ANCIENT ORIENTAL MONARCHIES, cloth, 1s.; Part II., GREECE AND ROME, cloth, 2s.; Part III., MEDIÆVAL HISTORY, cloth, 1s.; Part IV., MODERN HISTORY, cloth, 2s. 6d.

"Surpasses most of its predecessors in usefulness."—**Westminster Review.**

HISTORY—*Continued.*

An Epitome of History, ANCIENT, MEDIÆVAL, and MODERN. For Higher Schools, Colleges, and Private Study. By CARL PLOETZ. Translated by W. H. TILLINGHAST. 630 pp., post 8vo, cloth, 7s. 6d.

A Synopsis of English History: or, HISTORICAL NOTE-BOOK. Compiled by HERBERT WILLS. 144 pp., crown 8vo, cloth, 2s.

Our Country: A History for Lower Forms. By the Rev. EDGAR SANDERSON, M.A., Clare College, Cambridge. Fully Illustrated. Crown 8vo, cloth, 1s. 4d.

The Story of England: A History for Lower Forms. By the Rev. EDGAR SANDERSON, M.A., Clare College, Cambridge. Fully Illustrated. Crown 8vo, cloth, 1s. 6d.

The two volumes *Our Country* and *The Story of England* are complementary of each other. Each traverses the field of English History, but the first deals at greater length with the early history, and touches more fully upon the romantic episodes than the other. The two serve well to attract beginners to read English History, and to give them a broad foundation upon which to build.

The Scots Reader: A History of Scotland for Junior Pupils. By DAVID CAMPBELL, Headmaster of the Academy, Montrose. Profusely Illustrated. Cloth, 1s.

The Century Historical Readers: Edited by THOMAS ARCHER and the Rev. EDGAR SANDERSON, M.A. Illustrated with Pictures, Maps, Portraits, &c.; strongly bound in cloth. These Readers tell the story of England in bright simple narratives and biographical notices.

BOOK I. & II. SIMPLE STORIES, 8d. and 10d.

BOOK III. EARLY ENGLISH HISTORY, 1s.

BOOK IV. 1066–1485, 1s. 4d.

BOOK V. THE TUDORS, 1s. 6d.

BOOK VI. THE STUARTS, 1s. 6d.

BOOK VII. THE HOUSE OF HANOVER, 1s. 6d.

"Mr. Archer has apprehended the distinction between a reading-book and a cram-book. Instead of crowding his pages with names and dates he has written a simple and interesting narrative."—Journal of Education.

GEOGRAPHY.

Blackie's Descriptive Geographical Manuals. By W. G. BAKER, M.A.

The series takes up the subject of Geography in sections and treats it on broad principles. The endeavour has been made to give a reasonably complete idea of the countries of the world, the manners and

GEOGRAPHY—*Continued*.

customs of the inhabitants, &c. Good descriptive matter, selected from the works of travellers, and profuse pictorial illustration give a living interest to the subject. The series consists of five volumes, namely:

No. 1. REALISTIC ELEMENTARY GEOGRAPHY. Taught by Picture and Plan. Embracing Direction, The Elements of Maps, Definitions, &c. The Pictorial Examples are derived chiefly from the Geographical Features of England. Crown 8vo, cloth, 1s. 6d.

No. 2. THE BRITISH EMPIRE. PART I.—The Home Countries: England, Wales, Scotland, and Ireland. With 7 Coloured Maps, &c. Crown 8vo, cloth, 2s.

No. 3. THE BRITISH EMPIRE. PART II.—The Colonies and Dependencies. With 6 Coloured Maps and numerous Illustrations. Crown 8vo, cloth, 2s.

No. 4. EUROPE (except the British Isles). Crown 8vo, cloth, 2s.

No. 5. THE WORLD (except the British Possessions). Crown 8vo, cloth, 2s.
[*In preparation.*

THE GEOGRAPHY OF THE BRITISH EMPIRE. Complete. The above Parts I. and II. in one volume. Crown 8vo, cloth, 3s. 6d.

Zehden's Commercial Geography of the World: Chief Centres of Trade and Means of Communication, Natural Productions, Exports, Manufactures, &c. Translated from the German of Professor ZEHDEN, Handelsakademie, Leipzig. With Map of the Chief Trade Routes. *Second Edition*, corrected to date, 592 pages, crown 8vo, cloth, 5s.

Australasia; A Descriptive Account of the Australian and New Zealand Colonies, Tasmania, and the adjacent lands. By W. WILKINS. Fully Illustrated. Crown 8vo, cloth, 2s. 6d.

A Pronouncing Vocabulary of Modern Geographical Names, nearly ten thousand in number; with Notes on Spelling and Pronunciation, &c. By GEORGE G. CHISHOLM, M.A., B.Sc., Author of "A Handbook of Commercial Geography". F'cap 8vo, cl., 1s. 6d.

A Synoptical Geography of the World: A Concise Handbook for Examinations, and for general reference. With a complete series of Maps. Crown 8vo, cloth, 1s.

The Geography of North America: A brief handbook for students. With synopses and sketch maps. Cloth, 6d.

The Geography of Asia: A brief handbook for students. With synopses and sketch maps. Cloth, 6d.

The Century Geographical Handbooks: Clearly arranged synopses, with many sketch maps and coloured maps.

No. III.—ENGLAND. 16 pp., 2d.

No. IV.—BRITISH ISLES, BRITISH NORTH AMERICA, AND AUSTRALASIA. 40 pp., 3d.

GEOGRAPHY—*Continued.*

No. IV.A-B.—SCOTLAND, IRELAND, CANADA, UNITED STATES, &c. 3d.

No. IV.C.—EUROPE, BRITISH NORTH AMERICA, AUSTRALASIA. 48 pp., 3d.

No. V.—EUROPE. 48 pp., 3d.

No. VI.—BRITISH COLONIES AND DEPENDENCIES. CLIMATE, INTER-CHANGE OF PRODUCTIONS. 40 pp., 3d.

No. VII.—UNITED STATES. OCEAN CURRENTS, &c. With 2 Coloured Maps. 3d.

No. VII.B.—THE WORLD, WITH EXCEPTION OF EUROPE. 4d.

"Nothing could exceed the judgment with which, from the vast storehouses of geographical knowledge, the salient points are picked out and set forth in these handbooks."—School Board Chronicle.

The Century Geographical Readers.

The aim of this series is to give a thoroughly readable account of the various countries of the world, and to stir the imaginations of the pupils by picturing the different peoples in their homes and occupations. The books are written in broadly descriptive and picturesque style. To aid the memory, a full, clearly-arranged tabular synopsis of the geographical facts is appended to each book. The books are profusely illustrated with pictures, plans, and maps, and are strongly bound in cloth.

No. I.—PLAN OF SCHOOL AND PLAYGROUND. Cardinal Points. Map. 8d.

No. II.—SIZE AND SHAPE OF THE WORLD. Geographical Terms. Physical Geography of Hills and Rivers. 10d.

No. III.—ENGLAND AND WALES. 1s.

No. IV.—BRITISH ISLES, BRITISH NORTH AMERICA, AND AUSTRAL-ASIA. 1s. 4d.

No. V.—EUROPE, Physical and Political, Latitude and Longitude, Day and Night, The Seasons. 1s. 6d.

No. VI.—BRITISH COLONIES AND DEPENDENCIES, Interchange of Productions, Circumstances which determine Climate. 1s. 6d.

No. VII.—UNITED STATES, Tides and Chief Ocean Currents. 1s. 9d.

Also Alternative or Supplementary Volumes:

No. IV.A-B.—BRITISH ISLES, BRITISH NORTH AMERICA, UNITED STATES. Day and Night, Air, Rain, Mist, Frost, &c. 1s. 4d.

No. IV.C.—EUROPE, BRITISH NORTH AMERICA, AND AUSTRALASIA. 1s. 6d.

No. VII.B.—THE WORLD, with exception of Europe. 1s. 9d.

THE WORLD, in one Volume. 1s. 6d.

"Messrs. Blackie are to be congratulated on the production of these works. It is difficult to imagine anything that the compiler has not done to make the subject as interesting as possible to youth."—Glasgow Herald.

ARITHMETIC.

A Systematic Arithmetic. By A. E. LAYNG, M.A., Headmaster of Stafford Grammar School. In Two Parts. Part I. now ready, extending to Decimals and the Unitary Method. Price 2s. 6d.; with Answers, 3s. The Bookwork separately, 1s. 6d. The Exercises separately, 1s.

This is distinctively a *new arithmetic.* The aim of the author has been to present a complete and lucid treatment of the arithmetical rules, with full and novel explanations and abundant illustrative examples, allotting to each rule space proportionate to its importance. The bookwork is kept entirely separate from the exercises, and each section is arranged so that it begins on a fresh page. Special care has been devoted to the preparation of the exercises, the principle of selection being to provide sufficient examples for practice without increasing merely mechanical labour.

PART II. will treat of Interest, Stocks, Shares, and the other branches of more advanced arithmetic.

Pickering's Mercantile Arithmetic, for Commercial Classes. By E. T. PICKERING, formerly Lecturer on Mercantile Arithmetic at the Birmingham and Midland Institute. Cloth, 1s. 6d.

"A most useful supplement to ordinary school arithmetics, and provides a course of work which will fit a youth for commercial life. The explanation of foreign exchanges is very good. We know of no book in which the matter is at once so full and so clear."—**Teachers' Monthly.**

MATHEMATICS.

Euclid's Elements of Geometry. With Notes, Examples, and Exercises. Arranged by A. E. LAYNG, M.A., Headmaster of Stafford Grammar School; formerly Scholar of Sydney Sussex College, Cambridge. BOOKS I. to VI., with XI., and Appendix; and a wide selection of Examination Papers. Crown 8vo, 3s. 6d.

BOOKS I. to IV. in one vol., 2s. 6d. BOOK I., 1s.; II., 6d.; III., 1s.; IV., 6d.; V. and VI. together, 1s.; XI., 1s. 6d.

KEY to BOOK I., 2s. 6d.; to complete Euclid, 5s.

The system of arrangement allows enunciation, figure, and proof to be all in view together. Notes and Exercises are directly appended to the propositions to which they refer.

"The special features of the work are the use of symbols, great clearness in the arrangement of the argument, and the exercises at the end of each proposition, which are those of a practical teacher who knows the capacity of the ordinary school-boy's intelligence. Those on the definitions are specially good, and will prove most suggestive."—**Spectator.**

MATHEMATICS—*Continued.*

Preliminary Algebra. By R. WYKE BAYLISS, B.A., Vice-principal of the United Service Academy, Southsea, formerly Scholar and Prizeman of Peterhouse, Cambridge. 2s.

"The explanations are brief but clear, and the exercises thereon abundant. Some extremely neat and novel methods of solving problems are here introduced to us."—Academic Review.

Algebra. UP TO AND INCLUDING PROGRESSIONS AND SCALES OF NOTATION. By J. G. KERR, M.A., Headmaster of Allan Glen's Technical School, Glasgow. F'cap 8vo, cloth, 2s. 6d.

"A well-arranged, clear, and useful little book."—Athenæum.

Algebraic Factors. HOW TO FIND THEM AND HOW TO USE THEM. Factors in the Examination Room. By Dr. W. T. KNIGHT, Headmaster Towcester School. F'cap 8vo, cloth, 2s. KEY, 3s. 6d.

"Invaluable to young students."—School Guardian.

Elementary Text-Book of Trigonometry. By R. H. PINKERTON, B.A., Balliol College, Oxford. F'cap 8vo, cloth, 2s.

"An excellent text-book. The exposition and demonstration of principles are remarkable for clearness and fulness."—Athenæum.

Mathematical Wrinkles for Matriculation and other Exams. By Dr. W. T. KNIGHT, Headmaster Towcester School. F'cap 8vo, cloth, 2s. 6d.

An Introduction to the Differential and Integral Calculus. With examples of applications to Mechanical Problems. By W. J. MILLAR, C.E. F'cap 8vo, cloth, 1s. 6d.

SCIENCE.*

NEW VOLUMES.

Deschanel's Natural Philosophy. AN ELEMENTARY TREATISE. By Professor A. PRIVAT DESCHANEL, of Paris. Translated and edited by Professor J. D. EVERETT, D.C.L., F.R.S. *Thirteenth Edition,* thoroughly revised and much enlarged. Medium 8vo, cloth, 18s.; also in Parts, limp cloth, 4s. 6d. each.

Part I.—Mechanics, Hydrostatics, &c. | Part III.—Electricity and Magnetism.
Part II.—Heat. | Part IV.—Sound and Light.

"Probably the best book on experimental physics we possess."—Academy.

"Systematically arranged, clearly written, and admirably illustrated, it forms a model work for a class in experimental physics."—Saturday Review.

"We have no work in our scientific literature to be compared with it."—Quarterly Journal of Science.

⁎⁎ A special detailed Catalogue of Scientific and Technical Works will be sent post free on application.

SCIENCE—*Continued.*

A Text-Book of Organic Chemistry. By A. BERNTHSEN, Ph.D., formerly Professor of Chemistry in the University of Heidelberg. Translated by GEORGE M'GOWAN, Ph.D. *New Edition, thoroughly revised and much enlarged.* Crown 8vo, cloth, 7s. 6d.

"This excellent treatise has been admirably translated, and a very useful addition has been made to the English scientific student's library. As far as we have tested it is accurate, and it is certainly sensible in arrangement, and lucid in style."—Lancet.

"Sure to take as high a place among the elementary text-books of organic chemistry in the English language as it has already done in the Fatherland."—Nature.

A Text-Book of Solid or Descriptive Geometry. By ALEX. B. DOBBIE, B.Sc., Assistant to the Professor of Civil Engineering and Mechanics, Glasgow University. Crown 8vo, cloth, 2s. 6d.

In this book pictures are introduced in order to smooth the way for the beginner. The book is clearly arranged in sections, and a large number of problems are given in full, with carefully-drawn diagrams.

"An excellent little book."—School Guardian.

"The modes of projection employed in this work contribute much to a clear conception of the principles involved."—Science and Art.

"A little book possessing many good points, and one upon which great pains have evidently been spent. There are about 350 diagrams in the book."—Nature.

Heat, and the Principles of Thermodynamics. By C. H. DRAPER, D.Sc., B.A. With many Illustrations. Cloth, 4s. 6d.

This book is divided into two parts. The first part contains an account of the chief experimental phenomena that result from the application of heat to matter; the second is devoted to the consideration of heat as a form of energy, and is written mainly for non-mathematical students.

"We heartily congratulate Dr. Draper on his book, and trust that it may meet with the success that it deserves."—Journal of Education.

"Dr. Draper has produced an excellent introduction to the subject. Illustrative examples abound."—Oxford Magazine.

Hydrostatics and Pneumatics. By R. H. PINKERTON, B.A., Balliol College, Oxford. Fully Illustrated. Cloth, 4s. 6d.

The aim of the author is to give an account of the fundamental principles of the subject such as can be understood without advanced mathematical knowledge. The book includes chapters on Units, Uniform Circular Motion, and Harmonic Motion, and very numerous illustrations and examples.

"A good and complete work on the subject. It is a successful attempt to produce a book suitable for students who have not been through a course in mechanics. . . . We have no hesitation in recommending this work."—Journal of Education.

"As is usual throughout this excellent science series, every effort is made to assist the student by the adoption of the simplest language and by leaving no point unexplained."—Daily Chronicle.

An Elementary Text-Book of Anatomy. By HENRY E. CLARK, Fellow of the Faculty of Physicians and Surgeons of Glasgow; Professor of Surgery in St. Mungo's College, Glasgow, &c., &c. Crown 8vo, cloth. [*Nearly ready.*

SCIENCE—*Continued.*

The Student's Introductory Handbook of Systematic Botany. By JOSEPH W. OLIVER, Lecturer on Botany, Birmingham Municipal Technical School. Illustrated. Cloth, 4s. 6d.

"This little book fulfils in a very excellent manner the main requirements of a student's text-book. . . . The book is copiously and well illustrated . . . calculated to be of great service, and we can most cordially recommend it."—*Oxford Magazine.*

"Unquestionably the best introduction to systematic botany that has yet been published."—*Gardeners' Magazine.*

Elementary Metallurgy. By W. JEROME HARRISON, F.G.S., Chief Science Demonstrator, Birmingham School Board, and W. J. HARRISON, junr. Fully illustrated. Cloth. (*In preparation.*)

Elementary Text-Book of Physics. By Prof. EVERETT, D.C.L., F.R.S. F'cap 8vo, cloth, 3s. 6d.

"After a careful examination we must pronounce this work unexceptionable, both in the matter and the manner of its teachings."—*Journal of Science.*

Outlines of Natural Philosophy. By Professor J. D. EVERETT, D.C.L., F.R.S. F'cap 8vo, cloth, 4s.

"A book of great merit."—*Athenæum.*

Theoretical Mechanics. By R. H. PINKERTON, B.A., Balliol College, Oxford; Lecturer in Mathematics, University College, Cardiff. F'cap 8vo, cloth, 2s.

"Like all the works in the series this book is admirable. It is clear, concise, and practical, and well calculated to meet the purpose."—*Practical Engineer.*

Elementary Text-Book of Dynamics and Hydrostatics. By R. H. PINKERTON, B.A., Balliol College, Oxford, Lecturer at University College Cardiff, Examiner at Glasgow University. F'cap 8vo, cloth, 3s. 6d.

"The book leaves nothing to be desired."—*Nature.*

"Should prove most useful for science classes, and in schools and colleges."—*Invention.*

The Arithmetic of Magnetism and Electricity. By ROBERT GUNN. F'cap 8vo, cloth, 2s. 6d.

"Will be found very useful by advanced students, and is certain to have an excellent effect on the accuracy of their work."—*University Correspondent.*

Magnetism and Electricity. By W. JEROME HARRISON and CHARLES A. WHITE. F'cap 8vo, cloth, 2s.

"We should award this volume a high place among books of its class. The chapter on 'Potential' is specially to be commended."—*Education.*

Light, Heat, and Sound. By CHARLES H. DRAPER, D.Sc.(Lond.), Headmaster of Woolwich High School. F'cap 8vo, cloth, 2s.

"We can cordially recommend this book. It is well printed and neatly illustrated, and the statements are clear and accurate."—*Practical Teacher.*

SCIENCE—*Continued.*

Elementary Inorganic Chemistry: THEORETICAL and PRACTICAL. With examples in Chemical Arithmetic. By A. HUMBOLDT SEXTON, F.R.S.E., F.I.C., F.C.S., Professor of Metallurgy, Glasgow and West of Scotland Technical College. F'cap 8vo, cloth, 2s. 6d.

"Chemical Physics and Arithmetic receive a greater amount of attention than is usual in such books; and the exercises, experiments, and questions are well selected."—National Observer.

Chemistry for All, or Elementary Alternative Chemistry in accordance with the Science and Art Syllabus. By W. JEROME HARRISON, F.G.S., and R. J. BAILEY. F'cap 8vo, 1s. 6d.

"The matter contained in the book is accurate, well arranged, and tersely expressed. The majority of the diagrams are remarkable for the absence of unnecessary detail, and are such as the learner may be reasonably required to reproduce. We can recommend this Chemistry as one of the best, if not the best, of its kind we have seen."—Journal of Education.

Qualitative Chemical Analysis, INORGANIC and ORGANIC. By EDGAR E. HORWILL, F.C.S., Lecturer in Chemistry at the Battersea Pupil Teachers' Centre, &c. F'cap 8vo, cloth, 2s.

An Elementary Text-Book of Physiology. By J. M'GREGOR-ROBERTSON, M.A., M.B., Lecturer in Physiology, Queen Margaret College. *New and Revised Edition.* F'cap 8vo, cloth, 4s.

"A good system of arrangement and clear expressive exposition distinguish this book. Definitions of terms are remarkably lucid and exact."—Saturday Review.

Elementary Physiology. By VINCENT T. MURCHÉ. F'cap 8vo, cloth, 2s.

"We can confidently recommend this most admirable work."—British Medical Journal.

Earth-Knowledge. A TEXT-BOOK OF PHYSIOGRAPHY. By W. JEROME HARRISON, F.G.S., and H. ROWLAND WAKEFIELD. 388 pages. F'cap 8vo, cloth, 3s. Also in Two Parts: Part I. 1s. 6d.; Part II. 2s.

"There can be no doubt about the usefulness of the book . . . it is excellent."—Nature.

Elementary Botany. By JOSEPH W. OLIVER, Lecturer on Botany and Geology at the Birmingham and Midland Institute. F'cap 8vo, cloth, 2s.

"May without exaggeration be pronounced to be one of the best of our existing elementary treatises on botany."—Midland Naturalist.

An Elementary Text-Book of Geology. By W. JEROME HARRISON, F.G.S., Joint-Author of "Earth-Knowledge", &c. F'cap 8vo, cloth, 2s.

"The best text-book, in this branch of science, for the beginner, we have yet come across."—Literary World.

An Elementary Text-Book of Applied Mechanics. By DAVID ALLAN LOW (Whitworth Scholar), M.Inst.M.E. F'cap 8vo, cloth, 2s.

"An excellent little text-book."—Nature.

SCIENCE—*Continued.*

Elementary Agriculture. Edited by R. P. WRIGHT, Professor of Agriculture, Glasgow and West of Scotland Technical College. F'cap 8vo, 1s. 6d.

"It is as useful and trustworthy a little treatise of the kind as we have seen."—Nature.

Elementary Hygiene. By H. ROWLAND WAKEFIELD, Science Demonstrator, Swansea School Board, Joint-Author of "Earth-Knowledge", &c. F'cap 8vo, 2s.

"Contains a large amount of information, conveyed in clear and precise terms."—British Medical Journal.

SCIENCE FOR BEGINNERS.

Chemistry for Beginners. By W. JEROME HARRISON. 144 pages, cloth, 1s.

Agriculture for Beginners. Edited by Professor R. P. WRIGHT. 144 pp., cloth, 1s.

Botany for Beginners. By VINCENT T. MURCHÉ. 144 pp., cloth, 1s.

Magnetism and Electricity for Beginners. By W. G. BAKER, M.A. 144 pp., cloth, 1s.

Mechanics for Beginners. By DAVID CLARK. 220 pp. Cloth, 1s. 6d.

Animal Physiology for Beginners. With coloured Illustrations. By VINCENT T. MURCHÉ. 144 pp., cloth, 1s. 6d.

Science Readers. Fully illustrated, strongly bound in cloth. The lessons in this series of Readers are designed to awaken interest in the common objects of the natural world, and give pupils some insight into the processes by which articles of common use are produced.

BOOK I.—TALES AND TALKS ON COMMON THINGS. Part I. 8d.

BOOK II.—TALES AND TALKS ON COMMON THINGS. Part II. 10d.

BOOK III.—THE YOUNG SCIENTISTS: SIMPLE PRINCIPLES OF CLASSIFI-CATION. Substances used in Arts and Manufactures. Phenomena of Earth and Atmosphere. Matter in Three States: Solids, Liquids, and Gases. 1s.

BOOK IV.—OUR FRIENDS OF THE FARM. By the Rev. THEODORE WOOD, F.E.S. 1s. 4d.

BOOK V.—ANIMAL AND PLANT LIFE. Part I. By the Rev. THEODORE WOOD, F.E.S. 1s. 6d.

BOOK VI.—ANIMAL AND PLANT LIFE. Part II. By the Rev. THEODORE WOOD, F.E.S. 1s. 6d.

"The idea is excellent, and has been very successfully worked out. The facts set forth have been carefully selected, and they are presented in a bright, easy, natural style, which cannot fail to make them at once intelligible and attractive. Good teachers will find the series of real service in helping them to foster in the minds of their pupils a love of accurate observation and independent reasoning."—Nature.

READING BOOKS.

FOR LOWER FORMS AND PREPARATORY SCHOOLS.

Readings from Standard Authors, &c.   Each foolscap 8vo, strongly bound in cloth.

THE SPECTATOR READER: Selections from Addison's Spectator. 1s. 3d.

READINGS FROM SIR WALTER SCOTT. 1s. 3d.

MARY QUEEN OF SCOTS: being Readings from THE ABBOT. 1s. 3d.

TALES FROM HENTY: being Selections from the Historical and other Romances of G. A. Henty. Illustrated, 1s. 6d.

THE CHARLES DICKENS READER. 1s. 4d.

THE SOVEREIGN READER: fully illustrated, forming a bright historical record of the events of Queen Victoria's reign. By G. A. HENTY. 1s. 6d.

THE CITIZEN: HIS RIGHTS AND RESPONSIBILITIES. By OSCAR BROWNING, M.A. 1s. 6d.

THE NEWSPAPER READER: Selections from the Journals of the Nineteenth Century. 1s. 6d.

THE BRITISH BIOGRAPHICAL READER. Sketches of Great Men selected from the Writings of Standard Authors. 1s. 6d.

READINGS FROM ROBINSON CRUSOE. Illustrated by GORDON BROWNE. 1s. 3d.

BLACKIE'S SHAKESPEARE READER. 1s.

Stories for the Schoolroom: edited by J. H. YOXALL. Illustrated by leading Artists; strongly bound in cloth. Selections from the works of authors who have proved themselves favourites with boys and girls. Among those represented are Baring-Gould, Manville Fenn, Harry Collingwood, George Mac Donald, Fenimore Cooper, Louisa Alcott, Alice Corkran, Amy Walton, George Sand (translated). The poetry is from Cowper, Wordsworth, Longfellow, Robert Browning, Lewis Carroll, Jean Ingelow, and old ballads.

"SPOT." For Infants. Cloth, 3d.

INFANT READER, 6d.

BOOK I., 8d.

BOOK II., 9d.

BOOK III., 1s.

BOOK IV., 1s. 4d.

BOOK V., 1s. 6d.

"We have here lengthy extracts from good authors, judiciously adapted and annotated. The tales are within the grasp of children, and cannot fail to entertain them. The type is clear, the illustrations good. A happy idea, ably worked out, we wish these Readers the success they well deserve."—Journal of Education.

The Century Readers. A graduated series of Reading Books. Well illustrated and strongly bound in cloth.

FIRST PRIMER, 2½d.

SECOND PRIMER, 3d.

INFANT READER, 6d.

READER I., 8d.

READER II., 8d.

READER III., 1s.

READER IV., 1s. 4d.

READER V., 1s. 6d.

READER VI., 1s. 6d.

"The Century Readers are most prepossessing in appearance. Paper and type are excellent, and we have rarely seen a prettier binding. The passages are well graduated, and those written expressly for the series are admirably simple and sometimes charming without degenerating into silliness."—Journal of Education.

. *A detailed list of Drawing and Painting Books
will be sent on application.*

DRAWING AND PAINTING.

Vere Foster's Drawing Copy-Books. With Instructions and paper to draw on. In 72 Numbers at 2d. *Complete Edition,* in Eighteen Parts at 9d. (Each part complete in itself.)

FREEHAND (20 numbers).
LANDSCAPE (12 numbers).
ANIMAL AND HUMAN FIGURE (16 numbers).

GEOMETRICAL DRAWING (10 numbers).
PERSPECTIVE, MODEL DRAWING, SHADING (14 numbers).

Vere Foster's Model Drawing. Cloth boards, 1s. 6d.

Vere Foster's Rudimentary Perspective. Cloth boards, 1s. 6d.

Vere Foster's Water-Colour Drawing-Books. With coloured facsimiles of original water-colour drawings, and hints and directions.

LANDSCAPE PAINTING FOR BEGINNERS. First Stage. Three Parts 4to, 6d. each; or one volume, cloth elegant, 2s. 6d.

LANDSCAPE PAINTING FOR BEGINNERS. Second Stage. In Four Parts 4to, 6d. each; or one volume, cloth elegant, 3s.

ANIMAL PAINTING FOR BEGINNERS. In Four Parts 4to, 6d. each; or in one volume, cloth elegant, 3s.

FLOWER PAINTING FOR BEGINNERS. In Four Parts 4to, 6d. each; or one volume, cloth elegant, 3s.

SIMPLE LESSONS IN MARINE PAINTING. In Four Parts 4to, 6d. each; or one volume, cloth elegant, 3s.

SIMPLE LESSONS IN LANDSCAPE PAINTING. In Four Parts 4to, 6d. each; or one volume, cloth, 3s.

SIMPLE LESSONS IN FLOWER PAINTING. Four Parts 4to, 6d. each; or one volume, cloth elegant, 3s.

STUDIES OF TREES. In Eight Parts 4to, 9d. each; or two volumes, cloth elegant, 4s. each.

BRITISH LANDSCAPE AND COAST SCENERY. In Four Parts 4to, 9d. each; or one volume, cloth elegant, 4s.

MARINE PAINTING. In Four Parts 4to, 9d. each; or one volume, cloth elegant, 4s.

LANDSEER AND ANIMAL PAINTING IN ENGLAND. By W. J. LOFTIE. Containing Eight Facsimiles of original paintings, and numerous illustrations of celebrated pictures by Sir Edwin Landseer, R.A., George Morland, H. W. B. Davis, R.A., Briton Riviere, R.A., and Walter Hunt. In Four Parts 4to, 1s. each; or one volume, elegantly bound, 6s.

REYNOLDS AND CHILDREN'S PORTRAITURE IN ENGLAND. By W. J. LOFTIE. With Reproductions of Celebrated Pictures by Sir Joshua Reynolds, Thomas Gainsborough, George Romney, Sir Thomas Lawrence, James Sant, R.A., and Sir J. E. Millais, Bart. In Four Parts 4to, 1s. each; or one volume, cloth elegant, 6s.

DRAWING AND PAINTING—*Continued.*

ADVANCED STUDIES IN FLOWER PAINTING. In Six Parts 4to, 9d. each; or one volume, cloth, 6s.

SKETCHES IN WATER-COLOURS. In Four Parts 4to, 1s. each; or one volume, cloth elegant, 5s.

ILLUMINATING. Nine Examples in Colours and Gold of Ancient Illuminating of the best periods. By W. J. LOFTIE, B.A., F.S.A. In Four Parts 4to, 9d. each; or one volume, cloth elegant, 4s.

"Everything necessary for acquiring the art of painting is here; the *facsimiles* of water-colour drawings are very beautiful."—Graphic.

⁎⁎ *A detailed List of Vere Foster's Writing Copies, and Specimen Copies, will be sent on application.*

WRITING.

Vere Foster's Writing Copy-Books. The principle upon which Mr. Foster's system of writing is based is that children should from the very first be taught a *current hand.* Experience has abundantly proven that pupils using his copies soon become fluent penmen, and acquire a clear and distinct formed hand of writing that does not need to be unlearned when they enter business or professional life.

ORIGINAL SERIES, in Seventeen Numbers, price 2d. each.

PALMERSTON SERIES, in Eleven Numbers, on fine paper ruled in blue and red, price 3d. each.

BOLD WRITING, OR CIVIL SERVICE SERIES, in Twenty-five Numbers, price 2d. each.

POYNTER'S DRAWING-BOOKS.

Poynter's South Kensington Drawing-Books. Issued under the direct superintendence of E. J. POYNTER, R.A., who has selected the examples for the most part from objects in the South Kensington Museum. The original Drawings have been made under Mr. Poynter's supervision by Pupils of the National Art Training School. Each book with Fine Cartridge Paper to draw on.

FREEHAND DRAWING FOR CHILDREN. Familiar Objects, Tools, Toys, Games, &c. Four Books, 4d. each; or one volume, cloth, 2s. 6d.

FREEHAND FIRST GRADE. Simple Objects, Ornament (Flat and Perspective). Six Books, 4d. each; or one volume, cloth, 3s.

FREEHAND ELEMENTARY DESIGN. Simple Forms, Leaves, and Flowers. Two Books, 4d. each; or one volume, cloth, 2s.

FREEHAND FIRST GRADE—PLANTS. Six Books, 4d. each; or one volume, cloth, 3s.

POYNTER'S DRAWING-BOOKS—*Continued.*

FREEHAND SECOND GRADE. Ornament (Greek, Renaissance, &c.). Four Books, 1s. each; or one volume, cloth, 5s.

ELEMENTARY HUMAN FIGURE. Four Books, 6d. each; or one volume, cloth, 3s.

> BOOK I.—MICHELANGELO'S "DAVID"—Features (Eye, Nose, etc.).
>
> BOOK II.—MASKS, from Antique Sculpture.
>
> BOOKS III. AND IV.—HANDS AND FEET, from Sculpture.

"Will be simply invaluable to beginners in drawing."—*Graphic.*

HUMAN FIGURE, ADVANCED. Three Books, imp. 4to, 2s. each; or one volume, cloth, 8s. 6d.

> BOOK I.—HEAD OF THE VENUS OF MELOS.
>
> BOOK II.—HEAD OF THE YOUTHFUL BACCHUS.
>
> BOOK III.—HEAD OF DAVID BY MICHELANGELO.

ELEMENTARY PERSPECTIVE DRAWING. By S. J. CARTLIDGE, F.R.Hist.S. Four Books, 1s. each; or one volume, cloth, 5s.

FIGURES FROM THE CARTOONS OF RAPHAEL: Twelve Studies of Draped Figures. With Descriptive Text, and Paper for Copying. Four Books, Imperial 4to, 2s. each; or one volume, cloth, 10s. 6d.

A SELECTION FROM THE LIBER STUDIORUM OF J. M. W. TURNER, R.A., for Art Students. Comprising Four Facsimile Reproductions in Mezzotint; 51 Facsimile Reproductions of the Etchings, and 37 Text Reproductions of the Finished Engravings. With Historical Introduction and Practical Notes. In Four Parts, square folio, 12s. 6d. each; or complete in Portfolio, £2, 12s. 6d.

BLACKIE'S
PICTURES FOR SCHOOL DECORATION
AND OBJECT LESSONS.

These Pictures have been produced by the highest style of Chromo-Lithography, and in the most artistic manner. Two Pictures are mounted on each board, and varnished and eyeletted ready for hanging up.

FIRST SERIES.
Mounted on Boards (15½ × 10½ inches). Price 1s. each.

FLOWERS.—By ADA HANBURY. 5 Cards of 10 Pictures.

TREES.—By J. NEEDHAM. 7 Cards of 14 Pictures.

FIGURES.—By Sir JOSHUA REYNOLDS, &c. 4 Cards of 8 Pictures.

ANIMALS.—By Sir EDWIN LANDSEER, &c. 4 Cards of 8 Pictures.

SECOND SERIES.
Mounted on Boards (14½ × 9½ inches). Price 9d. each.

FLOWERS.—By ADA HANBURY and ETHEL NISBET. 10 Cards of 20 Pictures

ANIMALS.—By S. T. DADD, &c. 6 Cards of 12 Pictures.

DICTIONARIES, &c.

Annandale's Concise English Dictionary. Literary, Scientific, Etymological, and Pronouncing. Based on Ogilvie's Imperial Dictionary. By CHARLES ANNANDALE, M.A., LL.D. *New Edition, revised and extended,* 864 pp., f'cap 4to, cloth, 5s.; Roxburgh, 6s. 6d.; half-morocco, 9s.

"Stands towards other dictionaries of the smaller character in the relation of the 'Imperial' to rival lexicons—in other words, it holds the 'premier' place."—Spectator.

"In clearness of type, in size, shape, and arrangement, the volume leaves nothing to be desired. Till Dr. Murray's great work is completed it is not likely to be superseded."—Journal of Education.

"We do not hesitate a moment to bestow upon the *Concise Dictionary* our very highest praise. It forms in truth a priceless treasury of valuable information. Every teacher should possess a copy."—Practical Teacher.

Blackie's Modern Cyclopedia of Universal Information. A Handy-book of Reference on all subjects and for all Readers. Edited by CHARLES ANNANDALE, M.A., LL.D., Editor of "Ogilvie's Imperial Dictionary", &c. Complete in Eight Volumes, 512 pp., cloth, 6s.; or half-morocco, 8s. 6d. each.

"Looking at the eight volumes as they stand side by side upon the shelf, we are bound to say that a more handsome and useful addition to a library, public or private, is not to be obtained. The money which the complete *Cyclopedia* costs could not be more sensibly laid out."—Review of Reviews.

"There is no subject of human interest that has been omitted so far as we have been able to discover. . . . As valuable a compendium of universal information as editorial experience and publishing enterprise could possibly achieve within the limits of eight not over bulky volumes."—The Daily Chronicle.

The Student's English Dictionary. For the use of Colleges and Advanced Schools. By JOHN OGILVIE, LL.D. Illustrated by 300 Engravings. Roxburgh, 7s. 6d.; half-calf, 10s. 6d.

A Smaller English Dictionary. Etymological, Pronouncing, and Explanatory. For the use of Schools. By JOHN OGILVIE, LL.D. Cloth, 2s. 6d.; Roxburgh, 3s. 6d.

Full Prospectus showing Specimen Pages of the above valuable Works of Reference will be sent free on application.

BLACKIE'S SCHOOL AND HOME LIBRARY.

Under the above title the publishers have arranged to issue for School Libraries and the Home Circle, a selection of the best and most interesting books in the English language.

In making a choice from the vast treasure-house of English literature the aim has been to select books that will appeal to young minds; books that are good as literature, stimulating, varied and attractive in subject-matter, and of perennial interest; books, indeed, which every boy and girl ought to know, and which, if once read, are sure to be read again and again.

The Library will include lives of heroes ancient and modern, records of travel and adventure by sea and land, fiction of the highest class, historical romances, books of natural history, and tales of domestic life.

School Managers, Teachers, and Parents may therefore confidently place the volumes in the hands of the children, in the assurance that they are giving them nothing but what is wholesome and refining.

The greatest care will be devoted to the get-up of the Library. The volumes will be clearly printed on good paper, and the binding made specially durable, to withstand the wear and tear to which well-circulated books are necessarily subjected.

NOW READY:

In Crown 8vo volumes. Strongly bound in cloth. Price 1s. 4d. each.

MISS MITFORD'S OUR VILLAGE.

MARRYAT'S CHILDREN OF THE NEW FOREST.

AUTOBIOGRAPHY OF BENJAMIN FRANKLIN.

LAMB'S TALES FROM SHAKSPEARE.

DANA'S TWO YEARS BEFORE THE MAST.

SOUTHEY'S LIFE OF NELSON.

WATERTON'S WANDERINGS.

ANSON'S VOYAGE ROUND THE WORLD.

SCOTT'S TALISMAN.

THE BASKET OF FLOWERS.

MARRYATT'S MASTERMAN READY.

LITTLE WOMEN. By L. M. ALCOTT.

COOPER'S DEERSLAYER.

PARRY'S THIRD VOYAGE,

DICKENS' OLD CURIOSITY SHOP. 2 VOLS.

PLUTARCH'S LIVES OF GREEK HEROES.

GOLDSMITH'S VICAR OF WAKE-FIELD.

WHITE'S NATURAL HISTORY OF SELBORNE.

To be followed by two volumes on the first of each month.

"The whole series may be placed in the hands of the rising generation with the utmost confidence. We feel sure that they will form a collection which boys and girls alike, but especially the former, will highly prize; for whilst they contain interesting, and at times very exciting reading, the tone throughout is of that vigorous, stirring kind which is always appreciated by the young."—Sheffield Independent.

"The series will be worthy the attention of all who are interested in village and school libraries."—Glasgow Herald.

Detailed Prospectus and Press Opinions will be sent post free on Application.

LONDON: BLACKIE & SON, LIMITED, 50 OLD BAILEY, E.C.
GLASGOW AND DUBLIN.

In Course of Publication.

To be completed in Sixteen Monthly Parts, imperial 8vo, price 2s. 6d. each, nett.
Also in Four Half-volumes at 12s. 6d. each, nett, or Two Volumes, 25s. each, nett.

THE
NATURAL HISTORY OF PLANTS
THEIR FORMS, GROWTH,
REPRODUCTION, AND DISTRIBUTION,

FROM THE GERMAN OF
ANTON KERNER VON MARILAUN,
Professor of Botany in the University of Vienna,

BY
F. W. OLIVER, M.A., D.SC.,
Quain Professor of Botany in University College, London,

WITH THE ASSISTANCE OF
MARIAN BUSK, B.SC., AND MARY EWART, B.SC.

**With about 1000 Original Woodcut Illustrations
and Sixteen Plates in Colours.**

KERNER'S NATURAL HISTORY OF PLANTS, now for the first time presented to English readers, is one of the greatest works on Botany ever issued from the press. Its province is the whole realm of Plant Life, and its purpose, as conceived by the author, Professor Kerner, of Vienna University, is to provide "a book not only for specialists and scholars, but also for the many".

To the preparation of the work Professor Kerner has devoted a quarter of a century of earnest labour, bringing to bear upon it the highest professional knowledge, experience, and skill. It is thus in nowise a sweeping together of current views, but has the rounded completeness of an original work of art; it might indeed be fitly named The Epic of Plant Life.

The work will be completed in 16 parts imperial 8vo, published monthly, at 2s. 6d. each, *nett*. Subscribers' names will be received by all booksellers.

Detailed Illustrated Prospectus, with Author's Note to the English Edition, and Sir John Lubbock's Opinion of the Work, will be sent on Application.

LONDON: BLACKIE & SON, LIMITED; GLASGOW & DUBLIN.